SELF-PACED SUSTAINABILITY

Reducing Impact on Your Terms

Dee M. Davis, TLP, CEM, LEED AP

ADVANCE PRAISE FOR SELF-PACED SUSTAINABILITY

Self-Paced Sustainability by Dee M. Davis is a powerful, relatable, and inspiring guide for anyone looking to integrate sustainability into their everyday life. Dee's candid storytelling, practical tips, and approachable strategies make what often feels like an overwhelming topic both accessible and enjoyable. Whether you're a sustainability novice or a seasoned eco-enthusiast, you'll find encouragement, actionable steps, and motivation to take meaningful action. This book proves to be a companion for the journey toward a more sustainable and fulfilling lifestyle. A must-read for anyone who wants to make a difference—starting one starfish at a time.

Connie Evans, DC

I absolutely love this book! The practical tips in each chapter are clear and actionable—easy to follow and start using right away. The "Hey Dee!" Q&A sections are brilliant. They address common questions and add a personal touch to the book. Overall, this is truly a great read!

Frank Shapour, PE

This book is a great tool to have in your toolbox. With Dee's coaching and expertise, anyone can read this book and feel capable of implementing a small change in their routine toward more sustainable habits. I especially appreciated the Beginner, Intermediate, Advanced summaries provided at the end of the chapters.

Lauren Taborda

The content of this book was well researched, and the narrative was so engaging, with such a personal voice, that it was like you and I discussing the subject over a cup of tea or a glass of wine! The text is sprinkled with humor throughout, and I found myself smiling or actually laughing out loud at some of your personal experiences. The subject of engaging in sustainability practices is broken down into chunks of ideas that everyone can embrace regardless of their level of commitment. When I finished the last page of the manuscript, a saying by Goethe came to mind, and thought it could and SHOULD be applied to Self-Paced Sustainability: "Whatever you can do, or dream you can, begin it."
Diane Antelline

This book covers such a wide variety of approaches to sustainability, along with tips on how to incorporate them into the average person's life without breaking the bank or being overwhelming.
Vickie Dunn

As the mother of two very young children, I am concerned about the chemicals used in my house and yard. Dee provides safe alternatives that I can trust for my family. I recommend her book to every parent interested in a chemical-free home!
Emily Rooney

The author's genuine passion for environmental stewardship shines through every page, making complex topics understandable and genuinely interesting. By focusing on progress over perfection, this book empowers readers to take meaningful steps toward a more sustainable lifestyle, one choice at a time.
Brian Traichel, Founder, My Target Client, Inc.
Las Vegas, NV

This book is a must-read for anyone looking to live more thoughtfully and leave a positive mark on the planet. It's incredible how reading a book makes you question the "little" things you do in life. Even if every reader just took one tip from this book – it already makes the world a more sustainable place. One starfish at a time! I love that Dee uses her life to share the message. This is the type of book that makes you a better person after reading it.

Michelle Shadpour, PE

This book is fantastic for someone who wants to implement ways to be more sustainable in their life. Whether your interest is in reducing the amount of plastics in your home, gardening, controlling pests, or saving water, there's a chapter for you. With easy to implement ideas, this book will help make sustainability attainable for all. Dee writes with a no judgement approach, giving everyone the encouragement to do something …because as she writes, even doing one thing can make a difference.   Sandra C. Gonzalez

Making a change in a person's life is always difficult, but when the reason for change is being more sustainable, most people cringe. Dee has done an excellent job showing how you can make a difference one small step at a time. Let's face it, our planet needs us all to be more self-conscious about how and what we do daily. Being more mindful of what we do daily doesn't mean we have to forgo our lifestyle; it only means we carefully consider our impact before you act. Dee has nailed it and trust me, you'll feel better for taking the first step.   L. R. Hering Sr., RADM, USN(ret)

Self-Paced Sustainability

Reducing Impact on Your Terms

Dee M. Davis, TLP, CEM, LEED AP

ISBN: 979-8-9913923-2-7

Copyright © 2025

Yellowstone Professional Education

All rights reserved. No part of this book may be copied, reprinted, or reproduced in any way, electronic or otherwise, without written permission from the author and/or publisher.

No warranties or guarantees are expressed or implied by the inclusion of the content herein. Neither the publisher nor the author shall be liable for any physical, psychological, emotional, financial, or commercial damages.

This publication includes the names of products, manufacturers, retail and online stores, and domain names, which may change over time. Neither the author nor the publisher accepts any liability for inaccuracies or misrepresentations. Neither the author nor the publisher are affiliated with or have received any compensation for their inclusion in this book. Recommendations and;/or references are based on personal opinion and experience. No guarantees are implied by their inclusion in this book.

Printed in the United States of America

TABLE OF CONTENTS

	Foreword by Jeffrey Klubeck	7
	Introduction	10
1	Start Where You Are	15
2	Recycling is Not the Answer	20
3	One Starfish at a Time…An Approach to Plastics	28
4	What the Fuzz? Low Hanging Fruit	49
5	Squirrel!	60
6	Start Bugging Your Bugs	71
7	Pets with Purpose	85
8	Now You're Cooking	95
9	The Lazy Composter	107
10	Happy Worms Make More Worms	128
11	Let's Get this Zero-Waste Party Started	135
12	Your Doomsday Dashboard	148
	Conclusion: Your Journey, Your Way	167
	Self-Paced Sustainability Resource List	169
	About the Author: Dee M. Davis	172

FOREWORD

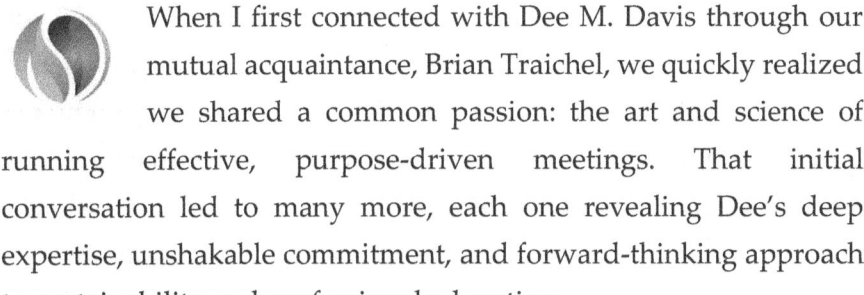When I first connected with Dee M. Davis through our mutual acquaintance, Brian Traichel, we quickly realized we shared a common passion: the art and science of running effective, purpose-driven meetings. That initial conversation led to many more, each one revealing Dee's deep expertise, unshakable commitment, and forward-thinking approach to sustainability and professional education.

As our discussions unfolded, I learned more about her drive to create meaningful change within industries that often struggle with efficiency and impact. I also saw firsthand her dedication to bridging the gap between technical knowledge and real-world application. This is a rare quality—one that turns ideas into action, and aspirations into tangible results.

It was this very dedication that led Dee to embark on the journey of writing *Self-Paced Sustainability: Reducing Impact on Your Terms*. I was surprised to learn Dee had been imagining and working on the book for nearly 20 years and absolutely honored when she invited me to coach her through completing the process, including access to my personal "Editor in Chief" for the guidance the project needed. As for the project itself...

This book is more than a guide; it is a call to action, offering readers a sustainable path forward that is not rigid or prescriptive but adaptable to their unique circumstances and values. To be thought of so highly by someone as accomplished as Dee and to be entrusted with the opportunity to contribute to this project is both humbling and immensely gratifying. I am deeply grateful for the chance to collaborate and add value where I could.

Given my background as a college professor of communication, a business and executive coach, and an author of multiple books on leadership, communication, and integrity, I recognize when a message is both timely and timeless. My work has always centered around motivation, accountability, and results, and I can confidently say that Dee embodies these principles in an extraordinary way. She is an educator, a leader, and a changemaker, and it is an absolute privilege to contribute to a project that aligns so well with my own values and professional mission.

Dee's extensive background in construction, engineering, and education, combined with her certifications as a Master Composter, Certified Energy Manager, and LEED AP, make her uniquely qualified to speak on sustainability. Yet, what truly sets this book apart is her ability to make the complex simple and the overwhelming achievable. She recognizes that sustainability is not a one-size-fits-all endeavor—it is a personal journey, one that each of us must navigate in our own way, at our own pace.

What I particularly love about this book is the way Dee makes sustainability fun. So often, conversations about environmental responsibility are riddled with guilt—guilt for not doing enough, for being unaware of all the options, or for feeling overwhelmed by the enormity of the challenge. But Dee takes all of that pressure off the table. She masterfully shifts the focus from obligation to opportunity, making sustainability an inviting and enjoyable pursuit. Her writing is engaging, insightful, and even humorous at times, making it easy to absorb her wisdom and put it into practice.

In a world where sustainability is often framed as an all-or-nothing pursuit, Dee's perspective is both refreshing and empowering. She invites readers to take meaningful steps without the pressure of perfection, demonstrating that small, intentional changes can lead to significant impact over time. Whether you are a business leader, a professional looking to integrate sustainability into your work, or simply someone who wants to reduce your environmental impact, this book provides the strategies and mindset shifts needed to make lasting progress.

As you turn these pages, I encourage you to embrace the concept of self-paced sustainability that Dee so brilliantly lays out. Let it challenge your thinking, spark new ideas, and inspire you to take action—on your terms, at your pace, with confidence. And most important, let yourself enjoy the journey.

Jeffrey Klubeck, M.A.
Founder/Author, The Integrity Game®
Lecturer, School of Communication, San Diego State University

INTRODUCTION

This book is for you, the average person that wants to live a more sustainable life but doesn't know where to start. Maybe you have started and are stuck, feeling overwhelmed by what to do next. Perhaps you have already taken several steps in your sustainability journey and are looking to do more. I was once you, and, really, I still am. No matter where you are on your journey, there is always more you can learn, more you can do. BUT WAIT—this is where the guilt and shame usually start to set in about not doing enough, but WE DON'T DO THAT HERE. You heard me, no guilt, no shame. This book is designed so you can achieve at YOUR pace. Whether you are a beginner, intermediate, or advanced sustainability achiever, you are an achiever; all you have to do is start somewhere, and guess what? YOU get to decide where, when, and how much you want to do.

The methods put forth in this book do not require you to spend a lot of money or radically change your life. In fact, many of these methods will save you money! Who doesn't like saving money? Now that you have decided to read on, congratulations on taking your next step to living a more sustainable life! A wise person once said,

"A journey of a thousand miles begins with a single step." I have found this is a very true statement. We are often deterred from accomplishing big things by looking at the whole picture all at once and never getting to the stage where we break it down into manageable steps that we can tackle. We are programmed to strive for perfection, so the fear of failure or feelings of overwhelm prevent us from trying something new if we are not sure we will master it quickly. I believe that the goal of any new venture is progress, not perfection. For that reason, I wrote this book so you can integrate sustainability inato your life at your pace. Depending on where you are on your journey, you can do as little or as much as you want. Do just one thing or delve deeper into what you are already doing—no judgment here! We learn from our mistakes and move forward, and, boy, have I made mistakes! I will gladly share my sustainability adventures with you, warts and all, to provide you with a shortcut to success in your sustainability journey.

Hello, I am Dee M. Davis, and I am passionate about sustainability. My journey has been unique and has evolved over the course of many years. What began as my parents' quest to save money and resources has become a way of life for me and my family and, by extension, many of my friends and students. With everything I have learned, I always seek to know more. As a result, I have become an avid student of sustainable living and have taken courses in topics like Conservation Psychology, Environmental Psychology, Recycling and Waste Diversion, Environmental Economics, and Sustainable Behavior Change. In turn, I share my knowledge, teaching courses in Composting, Energy Use, Vermicomposting, Water Reuse, and LEED (Leadership in Energy and Environmental Design) and have obtained certifications as a Master Composter, a Teaching and Leaning Professional, and a Certified Energy

Manager. I love to share what I have learned in the classroom and in life on social media and in my courses and podcasts.

Throughout the various stages of life and learning, my vision of sustainable living has evolved, as has my definition of sustainability. While the concept means different things to different people, I define sustainability primarily as reducing demand, consuming less, and preserving and reusing resources with the least amount of waste possible. It took decades for my journey to evolve into the life I live today; so, I know that it can be overwhelming for some to consider. Here you will discover that you don't have to take a giant leap and make a major lifestyle change to make a difference. The good news is that anyone can be sustainable by doing one thing, whether it is big or small, and implementing that practice in their daily life at work and at home.

In this book, I share many of the ways anyone can practice sustainability in their life. Whether you choose to focus on one thing or several things, there will always be more you can do, but please don't let that overwhelm you. You don't have to do it all! Finding one, two, or a few things that resonate with you is enough, and you can choose to start small or go all in. Sustainable living is a personal choice, driven by desire, necessity, accessibility, and convenience. Fear of judgment, guilt, or shame should never come into play.

The journey toward living a sustainable life is not a destination to be reached; it is an ongoing effort to reduce our overall impact, become more self-reliant, and save some money along the way. Regardless of how much you decide to do to reduce your impact, it begins with a single step. My goal is to help you take that first step and then, if you choose, your next ... and your next.

Let's get rid of the notion that sustainable living means you must get rid of everything you own and shift your life to the extreme. In this book, I hope to change that conversation. You can call yourself sustainable without changing everything you do or where you live. It is perfectly okay to take baby steps and make only the changes you want to make.

I realize that some options we discuss in the book might not pertain to you or be available in your area, and that's okay. Take the step that resonates the most with you and your lifestyle. Once that becomes a habit, add an additional step, and then another. Within each chapter, there are multiple options from which you can choose, depending on where you are on your journey, beginner, intermediate, or more advanced. The chapters themselves are organized with the easier items to implement in the first seven chapters, followed by the median-level implementation in chapters eight, nine, and ten, and the more advanced in chapters eleven and twelve. At the end of each chapter, there is a section called "Hey, Dee," where I answer common questions related to that chapter. If you have additional questions that are not answered in this book, please contact me at heydee@selfpacedsustainability.com.

You might also notice that this book includes sustainability measures that are commonplace, such as reducing plastics, while it also addresses some that are less common, such as solar cooking. I have intentionally included a broad spectrum of topics in the hope that everyone will find some that appeal to them, based on their lifestyle and interests. Whatever you choose, I encourage you to keep it simple. Doing too much at one time can be overwhelming; instead, do one thing at a time. Once you've mastered it, move on if you wish to the next level or include an additional way to create a more sustainable home, workplace, and life.

What you will NOT find in this book are big, expensive, or extreme concepts, changes, or products. I'm not going to tell you that you need to buy an electric vehicle and put solar panels on your house. I'm not going to tell you that you have to move to the boonies and get off the grid with a composting toilet. You absolutely can do these things, but that is not what this book is about. Self-paced Sustainability is about making small, progressive changes that can be implemented by everyone.

For me, on the days when I can teach a group how to compost, help set up a recycling program, or simply help someone reach for the recycle bin instead of the trash can, all the hard work is worth it. Each time I take one more step on my long journey toward living a more sustainable life, I know I am doing the right thing, and I have a ton of fun doing it! I hope that in these pages you can find some things you can do to live more sustainably and leave our beautiful planet a little bit better for it. And remember, you will never be on this journey alone. I'm right by your side, ready to show you the way.

Let's get started!

1 START WHERE YOU ARE

You must start where YOU are, and not where me or anyone else is in their journey. For those of you who are just getting started, welcome to the beginning of your journey! For those who have already embarked on creating a sustainable life, I encourage you to continue at your own pace. Please do not compare your beginning with someone else's middle, or this will seem an overwhelming task, and it absolutely is not. My journey continues, I am always learning, growing, and trying new things. Sustainability is a journey, not a destination!

For me, the idea of sustainability was integrated into my life during childhood, not out of a specific interest or drive, but out of necessity. My father spent over 40 years as an engineer for a local water district, so conserving water was always strongly stressed and often discussed when growing up. Do you know what an acre foot of water is? Most people don't, but I do! It is the volumetric measurement of an acre of water one-foot deep. That's 325,851 gallons or 43,559.9 cubic feet for most of us. Since water districts deal in large volumes of water, they often speak in acre-feet. I was taught to never leave the water running any longer than absolutely necessary to accomplish the task. I grew up in Southern California where water conservation is a particularly important topic. California imports more than 90% of the water they consume; they are highly populated and have a climate with very little rainfall. But I promise, we will not get into the politics of water in this book!

When I was very young, we lived in the city, but when I turned nine, my parents sold our house, and we moved to a rural home with a couple acres of land in the Southern California mountains. My parents were both civil servants and, though we were comfortable, did not have a lot of extra money, so buying their dream home resulted in the conservation of resources becoming a way of life.

The move from the city to a rural area caused us to change our habits and took us further away from stores and access to convenient shopping for food and supplies. The drive into town for groceries and other household needs was 30 minutes or more down a mountain. Therefore, a weekly trip to the grocery store turned into a monthly trip, where we bought in bulk. Not only did we stock up on staples and learn the fine art of freezing and preserving food, but we started gardening, as well. While we had never been a wasteful family, our perspective changed, and our efforts to conserve and preserve became very intentional. Our gardening included growing a lot of our own vegetables, such as tomatoes, peas, onions, and potatoes, and a wide variety of fruit. We almost never ate out and conserved every possible resource, reducing waste and pinching pennies at every turn. We never called it sustainable living; it was simply a way of life necessary to live in a beautiful place on a limited income. This was our normal, but I know some of our cost-saving measures may sound extreme to some. We found ways to save money or conserve resources on almost everything. When we took a shower, we got wet, turned the water off, soaped up, and turned the water back on to rinse—same with shampooing and conditioning our hair. No wasted water in our house! (Years later, I joined the Navy and guess how you shower on a ship? You got it! I was already well versed in water-conservation showering!) Everything had a purpose, and everything had a place. Even our animals had jobs, which we will discuss in more detail in chapter seven.

Simply put, I was raised with a waste-not, want-not approach to life; you don't waste money, time, effort, or resources. It has since spread into every aspect of my life from home to work and my businesses, ingrained into my very being so much that I don't think about it anymore. In the writing of this book, it had to be called to my attention several times that I bring sustainability into everything I do, and that is not so for everyone. It is so ingrained into my being it is just part of who I am, and it can be that way for you, too, with some applied practice!

In the 1970's, there were no recycling centers, but there was the grocery store. Soda still came in glass bottles, and you paid a deposit when you purchased it. That deposit was refunded when you returned the empty bottles to the store. The soda bottling companies would pick them up from the stores and sterilize and reuse them. (Cue in the Archie Bunker music – "Those were the days.") Cans became popular shortly thereafter, and that changed everything – recycling took on a whole new meaning when recycling redemption values were started, we will discuss that in more detail in the next chapter.

While our family did everything we could to reduce waste, we didn't compost—at least not in the true sense of the word. We had a small chicken wire bin, where we threw dry leaves. Not knowing better, I thought that was composting – it wasn't until later that I learned it was more like stockpiling. I suppose my parents did not know how to properly compost, but it was their attempt to reduce waste (instead of throwing it in the trash), which was always stressed. Because we lived in a remote area, my parents didn't pay for trash removal due to the cost. What we threw away was loaded into my dad's truck, and he took it to work every week for disposal.

My parents did a fantastic job teaching us to conserve resources, which prepared me very well for the years that I was on my own without a lot of money. I knew how to handwash clothes, hang them out on a line, repair clothes, and where to go to have shoes resoled. My mom even reused dryer sheets, soaking them in liquid fabric softener and hanging them to dry until they were ready to be used again. We had no air conditioning, but we had a well shaded house and natural ventilation. Heat was provided by a wood burning stove in the living room. (No this was not the 1800's; it was the 1980's!) The wood burning stove is still in that living room, but after all the kids moved out, my parents sprung for forced air heat and cooling. After all those years of sacrifice, who can blame them?

When I moved out of my parents' home, I left the cost saving and sustainability efforts behind and fell into the lifestyle of the average American. I still remember the first time I took a shower and left the water running the entire time—it was heaven! While there were still some things that stuck with me from my childhood, sustainability wasn't a high priority.

Not surprisingly, it was money that pulled me back into sustainable behavior. My husband and I divorced, and I found myself in a new position as a young single mother with a lot of financial responsibility. Suddenly, I was faced with the need to pinch pennies, just like my parents had. Thankfully, I knew exactly what to do! Like them, I did everything I could to cut costs, including washing our clothes in the bathtub and hanging them to dry when I didn't have quarters to put into the machines. Living in an apartment, I was not growing my own food, but I knew how to buy what I needed inexpensively, and I could get by with a very small grocery budget week to week, cooking all our meals at home.

Since then, I have become far more aware of areas where I can conserve, reuse, recycle, and preserve, whether it is money, natural resources, utilities, or waste. My sustainability journey has expanded from recycling to refusing to purchase products that are made of plastic and other disposable / single-use materials. I've even adapted my parents' trash reduction efforts, becoming a master composter and composting most of the waste that would otherwise end up in the recycling or other waste stream. As a result, there is rarely any trash produced in our house, to the point that it is difficult to find a trash bin, which is very intentional.

Today, I teach composting and waste reduction to others, and I continue to grow my own efforts, experimenting with new things each passing year. Here I remind you not to compare your beginning with my middle; this is a journey, not a destination. My journey has lasted a lifetime and continues. Choose what resonates with you, what applies to your lifestyle, and what is available in your village, city, or state. The point is that it all starts with one step, and if you take just one step, you've contributed to a more sustainable household, workplace, and planet.

2   RECYCLING IS NOT THE ANSWER!

You are probably surprised to read this, but it is true. It is difficult to talk about sustainability without addressing recycling, but it is important to acknowledge that recycling is more of a challenging problem than a solution. Don't get me wrong—I'm all for recycling, and I recycle anything that I can't avoid, reuse, repurpose, or compost. In fact, this is the very strategy I have adopted over the years when I am engaging in the purchase of any product.

Avoid, Reuse, Repurpose, Compost, Recycle, Landfill

Avoid is the mind shift that we must make first when it comes to managing our waste streams. If we never buy the thing that needs to be recycled, we don't have to find a way to dispose of it. Recycling is not the answer; it is the consequence of non-avoidance. We will talk more about the avoiding strategy in chapter three, but make no mistake, recycling is a waste stream. It requires the consumption of a tremendous amount of energy, water, fuel, and other resources to produce the product in the first place, transport it to point of sale, transport to point of use, then transport to the recycling point, that then utilizes much more energy, water, and resources to recycle ... and the cycle repeats. Regardless of how it happens, once we have the object in our possession, we want to dispose of it in the most responsible way possible. If we cannot reuse, repurpose, or compost, then we look to recycling.

Recycling poses significant challenges when discussed in broad terms. The availability of recycling is greatly varied across the US, and even within a single state, city, or town in the same area. For example, I lived in a medium-sized city outside Denver where curbside recycling was available only to people living in apartments or townhomes, not private residences. A couple of towns away, curbside recycling was available to everyone, and a couple of towns in the other direction, recycling was only available if the residents brought their items to a recycling center. In some rural areas of the country, trash pickup is not even available, let alone recycling. What do people do with their trash and recyclables? Typically, they are put in trash piles or barrels and are then burned. I have been in towns that have "burn days," a designated day that everyone burns their trash in that area. Black smoke can be seen emanating from these burning piles, while melting plastics and metals off gas dangerous chemicals. It is easy to condemn someone for doing that, but what choice do they have with no trash pickup or recycling options? It should also give us pause to think about the process of recycling plastics—heat is applied to melt the plastic, then they are dried and formed into pellets (resulting in dangerous off gassing) that are then used for other products, where they are re-melted (more off gassing) into a new product.

When and where recycling is available, the type of waste that individual companies will accept can vary greatly. Some only accept certain types of plastic, while others pick up cardboard and paper products. Still others might accept aluminum or glass, while others refuse to accept those products. There are even some companies that give their customers mixed use recycling, throw it all in one bin, and they'll separate it out for you. That is best if you can get it!

Recycling can be confusing for the consumer, so it is easy to get it wrong, and items that aren't recyclable or locally accepted get thrown into the bin. For instance, did you know that there are many types of plastic, and some are recyclable in certain areas, while others are not?

Additionally, glass can be tricky; some waste haul providers will accept all glass, some only clear, and some want them separated by color. Clear glass bottles are okay, while green or brown glass might be unacceptable. While most of us know that cardboard is usually safe to recycle, there are recycling companies that refuse cardboard or packaging that has come into direct contact with food products—the empty pizza box from your favorite pizza joint comes to mind.

Are you confused? You are not alone.

Now, if recycling appeals to you and you live where services are accessible, I encourage you to take advantage of it to the extent you need it. It's easy to get started. You'll need one or more recycling bins, depending on the rules in your area. If you are lucky enough to have mixed-use recycling, you'll only need one recycling container and you can throw it all in there. Otherwise, you may need multiple containers for separating recyclables, paper, aluminum, glass, etc. To determine your specific needs, refer to the guidelines established by your waste hauling company. You will usually have a choice of waste haul providers in a given area; check each one to see what their rates and recycling policies are. Believe it or not, in the same service area you can get very different answers. There are waste haul providers I refuse to use because they either won't recycle when it's available or they have such ridiculous policies it makes it unreasonable. Regardless, recycling should be cheaper than trash pickup and sometimes differs in frequency of pickup.

Things that are generally recyclable:

- Some plastics: Plastics are a mix of chemicals blended to achieve certain properties, and the recycling numbers we see inside the recycling triangle (usually on the bottom of the container) identify the type of plastic.

Recycling symbol	Abbreviated name	Long name	Examples (may vary)
1	PETE	Polyethylene terephthalate	Water bottles, food containers
2	HDPE	High density polyethylene	Sprayers, cleaning supply containers, medicine bottles
3	PVC	Polyvinyl chloride	Pipes, tubing, fencing
4	LDPE	Low density polyethylene	Grocery bags, produce bags
5	PP	Polypropylene	potato chips, medicine bottles, cereal box liners
6	PS	Polystyrene	Clamshells, to go containers, cups, flatware
7	OTHER	Other plastics	Lotions

- Things like potato chip bags, medicine bottles, and cereal box liners are likely #5 polypropylene, whereas plastic flatware, Styrofoam, and food clamshells are #6 polystyrene. Whatever they are made of, they will have a number one through seven to identify the type of recyclable plastic. Your area may or may not have facilities to recycle all seven types.

- Paper: Printer paper, newspaper, and magazines, cardboard, catalogs, cereal boxes, junk mail, wrapping paper. (Note: almost all paper products are compostable! See chapters nine and ten on composting and book me for in-person composting classes or on demand at www.yspe.co .)
- Glass: Bottles, containers, jars.

There may be some things that are not recyclable at all or will have special rules in your area:

1. Plastic grocery and produce bags should not be thrown in a standard recycling bin. Reuse as much as possible, but if you must throw them out, many stores have a collection box in front where consumers can drop off their used plastic grocery and produce bags for recycling. Best option: just say no to the bags and bring your own. See chapter three for lots more on this topic!
2. Plastic wrap film.
3. High-heat glass like Pyrex dishes and bakeware.
4. Cups with plastic or wax coating. Their plastic lids may or may not be recyclable, check the symbol.
5. Plastic to-go containers of various types: Hard plastic clamshell or foam may or may not be recyclable at all, some only in select areas. Look for the #6 or, better yet, avoid them.
6. Packing peanuts: Some are recyclable these days, but they can be a menace to contain (as anyone who has ever opened a box

that uses these can attest!). These would most likely be a #6, but I have even found some that are compostable! (Yes, I did add them to my compost bin to test it for myself, and they decomposed quickly.) Store in a bag for reuse the next time you ship or take it to your local shipping store. Most will take them and reuse them as long as they are clean.

Recycling at Your Pace

Beginner: Set yourself up with recycling service from your waste haul provider. Get the container(s) for inside your house and label them with what is acceptable for each bin (I use 13-gallon trash cans) and talk to the other members of your household about the new system. Be patient as everyone learns new habits. Don't get discouraged if you make mistakes!

Intermediate: Start on your *Avoid* journey and mindfully look at the products you purchase, and find alternate products that have less packaging, no packaging, and eliminate plastics where you can. Chapter three is a great place to start! Reuse and Repurposing can be a really fun journey—there are many Facebook groups and Pinterest boards where you can get creative ideas on what to do with products to give them a longer useful life.

Advanced: Deepen your *Avoid, Reuse, and Repurpose* practices and start to *Compost.* I absolutely love composting! Not only can you divert thousands of pounds of waste in your own backyard, but you can create healthy soil amendments and have so much fun doing it! Through all these practices, see how much you can divert from the landfill! See chapters nine and ten.

"Hey, Dee!"

Commonly-asked Questions

1. Hey, Dee: Do I have to throw out all my recyclables in a container because one thing is in there that does not belong?

    Great job spotting that thing that should not be in there, and no, you DO NOT have to throw everything out. If it is something messy like food, clean it up, rinse it off, and you are good to go. If it needs to go into a different bin, then put it in there.

2. Hey, Dee: What if I don't have room in my kitchen / pantry to put a recycle bin?

    Under the counter or in the garage are options. When forming new habits, it is best to have things out where they are visible and readily accessible. You can move them into a more visually pleasing area later if you need to.

3. Hey, Dee: My household keeps throwing things in the trash that should go in the recycling bin. What can I do?

    Change can be tough, expect it to take some time. Clear labeling is helpful, as well as communication that comes across the right way. Word labeling worked for my household (paper, cardboard, junk mail or bottles, cans), but pictures of what is acceptable are an option. Consider reducing trashcan availability in the area and moving trash cans to be less convenient than the recycling bin.

4. Hey, Dee: Do I really have to wash my recyclables?

    Well, yes and no. Things put in the recycling bin should not have food or liquids in them and, ideally, there should be no food on them, either.

Soapy baths are not necessary, but a quick rinse is a good idea to keep the waste stream and your recycle bin from becoming a stinky mess.

5. Hey, Dee: I don't have recycling readily available in my area. What can I do?

   Avoiding plastics whenever possible is your best strategy. Look for products that are made from paper or compostable materials. Reuse and repurpose plastics that you must purchase, and consider composting as an additional strategy for reducing your waste footprint, see chapter nine for details! I offer in-person or on-demand composting classes at www.yspe.co.

Avoid, Reuse, Repurpose, Compost, Recycle, Landfill

3 ONE STARFISH AT A TIME...
AN APPROACH TO PLASTICS

Everywhere we look, quick, easy and disposable is the name of the game. Whether we are stopping for coffee on the way to work or grabbing a meal on the go, plastic is the disposable of choice. People everywhere are drinking out of plastic water bottles and eating with plastic utensils, and when they are done, they are tossed in the trash without a second thought. To put it into context, did you know that the useful life of a single-use item like a fork or straw is less than 10 minutes?

The idea of eliminating plastic or even reducing it can seem like fighting a battle, considering the overwhelming volume of plastics in the world and around us. I often hear people say things like, "Why are we replacing plastic straws with paper when there are all these other bigger plastic things we aren't doing anything about?" My answer is this – this is a whale of a problem, and we are going to tackle it one thing at a time. If I had it all my way, I am not sure I would have started with straws, but no one asked me.

Did you know there are FIVE plastic islands floating in the ocean? The largest is between California and Hawaii and has been named "The Great Pacific Garbage Patch." It covers an estimated 1.6 MILLION kilometers for those of you who are literate in the metric system. For the rest of us, that is twice the size of Texas! Two hundred million metric TONS of plastics make their way into the ocean each year (oceanconservancy.org). Allow me to share my eye-opening experience witnessing this.

Around 2019, I was living in San Diego and working in Santa Monica, taking the train up on Mondays and returning home on Thursday or Friday. I love commuting by train—this commute is a brutal one by car, so the train was the perfect solution. This route is coastal, so there are a lot of beautiful views of the water and beaches, as well as some of the coastal towns and cities. As you approach Los Angeles, the view changes to a very congested city with large concrete canals that lead from neighborhoods to the ocean. Since there is very little rainfall in Southern California (Los Angeles average annual rainfall is 14.82" averaged between 1877 and 2024) (laalmanac.com/weather), the canals are dry most of the time. During that time, small trees and bushes can grow in the bottom. (To picture these large canals in LA, recall the scene from the original Terminator movie where John Connor was being chased by the Terminator on his motorcycle. Those are the very canals I'm talking about!)

Most of my trips were in dry weather, but one day it was raining, and I watched a very different scene unfold. I knew these plastic islands existed and many non-profits are working on cleaning them up, but I never understood how all the plastic got into the ocean. Like most people, I thought it was from third world countries, or ships illegally dumping the ocean. After all, we are responsible stewards in the US, right? That day I had an a-ha moment.

In coastal California when it rains, the rainwater runs down the streets and sidewalks, into the gutters on the street. (Have you seen those little signs on the street gutters with a fish that say, "Don't pollute, I live downstream?") Well, guess what? The ocean is exactly where that rainwater flows to, and all the trash that goes with it. The canals become mighty dirty water rivers with thousands of pounds of trash (much of it plastic) floating on top and being dumped straight into the ocean. I was devastated to discover that the state I was born in and had lived in for much of my life in was contributing to the problem in such a massive and irresponsible way. I was equally devastated to realize that we in America are a significant part of the problem—it is much more convenient to think that third-world countries or someone else is the problem.

This is one state in the US. What about all the other coastal states, are they doing the same? What about other countries? I don't know, but it is on my list for research. The inland states don't have this option. Based on limited research, at least some of them are capturing the runoff, treating it, and using it for drinking water, which makes a metric ton of sense to me!

Now that I have scared you to death and given non-Californians another reason to despise the land of fruits and nuts, you might be thinking this is too big of a problem, what can I do about it? How can I possibly make a difference? In discussing this with my friend, Jeff, he reminded me of the Tale of the Starfish. A young girl is walking on the beach where a storm has washed up thousands of starfish. She began picking them up one by one and tossing them back into the ocean. Other people on the beach were watching her with amusement. An old man asked, "Why are you bothering? There are too many, you can't possibly make a difference." She smiled, picked up another and tossed it back into the ocean. "I made a difference for that one," she replied. The old man thought about it for a moment, smiled, and joined her in returning the starfish to the sea. Soon, other onlookers joined in, and all the starfish were returned to the water (story adapted from The Star Thrower by Loren C. Eisley[1]). Much like that little girl and her new friends, you and I will make a difference every day with every choice we make.

Step One: Look around and take inventory

Whenever I'm teaching a class on most any topic, one of the first things I ask my students to do is to look around and notice how many things they can see that are made of plastic. I ask you to look around you right now. What do you see? As I sit here writing this, there is plastic on my laptop, keyboard, monitor, and mouse. My cell phone, sunglasses, lotion container, lip balm, and the pen on my desk. Even my reading glasses are plastic. Plastic is so prolific in our everyday environment that we don't even see it anymore; it's simply a part of our everyday life.

Now look a little further – go into the kitchen, look in the fridge, the pantry, the cupboards. Next the bathroom, look under the sink. Laundry room, bedrooms, living room. Pay attention to what you have in your home that comes in a single-use container that is intended for you to use it once and dispose of it, only to buy another. Some of those things might be beverage bottles and cans, cleaning products, laundry soap, shampoo and conditioner bottles, liquid soap containers, dishwashing soap containers, plastic flatware, plastic cups, straws, and plates.

---

[1] "The Star Thrower" from THE UNEXPECTED UNIVERSE by Loren C. Eisley. Copyright ©1968 by Loren Eisley and renewed 1966 by John A. Eichman, III. Houghton Mifflin Publishing Company.

Now, think about what you bring into your house regularly or use and throw away while you are out. Takeout containers, single-use flatware, coffee cups, drinks on the go? This is not a guilt exercise, just a pause to look around you and think about this topic in relation to your daily life. This conscious effort will help you understand where to best start taking your first bite out of the whale.

Step 2: Limit or eliminate single-use bottles and cans

Single use – the world was not born this way! We know where we are now on this topic, and we know that we must understand our history to learn from it. I often conclude that the answer to many of the sustainability problems we face in today's world lies in the past. Asking ourselves, "How did we used to do it?" often gives us the answer we seek or gets us very close to it. When I was a kid, water came out of a tap, instead of a plastic bottle (the only water I recall buying at the store was distilled water), and beverages came in glass bottles. The consumer paid a deposit when they purchased the product, much like the redemption value we pay today, but today we pay the redemption value and we get only a small portion, if any, of it back. Some states don't have redemption values at all. Back in the day the full deposit was refunded to the customer when they returned their empty bottles to the store. The soda company would pick the bottles up from the stores and wash, sterilize, and reuse them. I have distinct memories of returning the bottles to the store with my dad and getting the deposit back. This was the OG of recycling!

In the early 1970s, aluminum cans replaced glass bottles, starting first with beer manufacturers, followed quickly by soda companies. Aluminum and plastic were regarded as easy and convenient for the consumer, and there was no need to return them to the store for recycling. What could be better? At this time, there were no consumer facing recycling programs in the United States. The history of bottling water goes back to Europe in the 1700's, but it did not become common practice in the United States until the late 1970's, when a big name soda brand started marketing bottled water, with marketing campaigns that led the consumer to believe the water was being sourced from pure mountain springs, when it was, in fact, sourced from municipal water supplies with added minerals. By the health crazed 1980's, several other brands entered the market, and by the 1990's, the misconception that municipal water supplies were not safe, and only bottled water was safe and healthy had stuck. It remains true today that most, if not all, commercial bottled water is sourced from the same municipal water supplies that come out of your tap at home for pennies on the dollar compared to bottled water. Bottling factories discovered their bottling production rates are about 10 times faster with plastic than with glass, breakage was no longer an issue, and the plastic was lighter. Production went up, transportation costs went down, and profits soared, so sustainable and reusable glass was doomed to become part of history. Today, over 50 billion plastic water bottles are produced every year (that is BILLION with a capital B). That's just water bottles, folks.

As we all know, the plastic industry isn't just for water, but includes many beverages and other containers. Metal cans that once housed aerosol sprays have been replaced with plastic for things like furniture polish, anti-perspirant, and hairspray. Plastic is now preferred by manufacturers over glass, paper, or cardboard for items like laundry detergent and trash bags. Our food and groceries aren't exempt from the plastic rage as it is now used for milk, to wrap produce and meat, package cheese, and provide convenient containers for products like pudding, yogurt, butter, and even our favorite childhood staples, peanut butter and jelly.

Options for limiting single-use bottles and cans:

1. **Adopt an emotional security water bottle!** You can check out mine on my You Tube Channel! When I realize I have left it at home, I am suddenly desperately thirsty and need it right now. Bottle filling stations are available in many places these days, and if you can't find one, you can (gasp!) fill it from a faucet. By the way – bottle filling stations and drinking fountains are tap water, folks. It might be chilled, but it's the same water that comes out of the tap. In my other life, I design and build utility systems in buildings, so believe me, it's the same water. Some may have filters, but I wouldn't count on it. If you have any concerns about tap water, there are many options for filters. Some water bottles have built-in filters, there are filtered carafes, point-of-use filters for your sink or whole home filters. Let's talk $$$$. Bottled water is 3,000% - 10,000% more expensive than tap water. Every time you buy a bottle of water, you agree to this markup, so the cost of filters if you prefer to use them is nothing in comparison to what you will save on the cost of water. According to studies from the Food and Water Watch, in developed countries, bottled water is no cleaner, safer or healthier than tap water[2].

   Did you know that more than 60 million disposable water bottles are thrown away every day? That equates to 22 billion

---

[2] reference https://svalbardi.com/blogs/water/bottled-vs-tap#:~:text=The%20main%20advantage%20of%20tap,per%20gallon%20of%20bottled%20water. Food and Water Watch who has numerous articles, studies and blogs on the topic.

plastic bottles a year! And every household can relate to water bottle waste. Just think about a handful of children and a case of bottled water. What happens? Within a few hours, partially filled water bottles cover the countertops and tables, only to be replaced with a new one because the bottles are forgotten, or the kids forgot which one was theirs. Providing filtered water in washable reusable cups can eliminate all that waste, expense ... and frustration! Think of how much money you will save when you stop buying cases of water every month!

2. **Make your reusable coffee cup your new travel companion.** Mine travels with me on planes, trains, and in automobiles. It goes with me to visit friends and family and attend conferences. Post COVID, you may still get the stink eye when asking a coffee shop to refill your own personal coffee mug, but they will usually do it. If they refuse, I will take my business elsewhere. Typically, they just act like the lid has the plague on it, but whatever. The most trouble I get into is in airport lounges. They want you to use a plastic disposable cup (noooo!!) to dispense the water or coffee into, then transfer it to your own cup. Since the design of both my coffee cup and water bottle are such that my mouth does not touch the part that is near (not touching) the dispenser, I usually just start with putting it directly into my own cup and see if anyone alerts the plastic police. I must confess I have a record and have been busted repeatedly at airport lounges across the country. I am convinced they give special training to the airport lounge employees on shaming customers when this sustainable behavior is spotted. I have been very loudly admonished for putting everyone at risk by not using a

disposable plastic cup because I clearly have cooties. Okay, they might not have used those words, but they are doing a great job publicly shaming people for sustainable behavior and creating a demand for single-use plastic. Once I witnessed a sustainable kinswoman refilling her water directly from the tap of the lounge water dispenser, and she was very loudly told that she was contaminating the entire container of water. They appeared to be very angry and removed the entire container to the kitchen, presumably dumped it, washed it, and refilled it before bringing it back out. The plastic police are getting really brazen; maybe they are getting kickbacks from the people who make those little plastic cups? I might call you for bail money one day when I finally get put in airport lounge jail for refusing to use a plastic cup.

3. **Reduce or eliminate purchasing of canned / bottled beverages.** At some point, I just stopped buying soda, Gatorade, tea, and other packaged beverages for my family. You know what happened? Nothing! Did they notice? Probably but there wasn't much fuss. I was prepared for a full-on family rebellion and frontal assault, complete with yelling and slamming doors, but nothing. Bottled beverages are full of sugar, chemicals, artificial colors and flavors, and they are expensive. BONUS: I saved a fair amount of money each month, and our family was contributing less waste to the environment!

4. **Reduce or eliminate the purchase of bottled water**. I remember buying it by the case, and I really don't know why or how this started. I remember all the waste from the kids

and their friends opening a bottle, taking a drink, setting it down—never finishing one before opening another. Our house was a sea of half-drained water bottles, and no one would claim them or finish them. The waste would infuriate me, until it occurred to me that I didn't have to do this. I could just stop buying them, and the problem would be solved, and again I would save money and fill the recycling bin a lot less. Are you noticing the trend of saving money here? It is a fallacy that making sustainable choices is expensive. There are options that cost money, some a lot of money, but most choices are no cost or cost saving! BONUS!!

Step 3: Shopping

1. **When shopping, choose foods that are not packaged in plastic whenever possible.** This is becoming increasingly difficult as it seems that stores are favoring putting everything in plastic. Have you seen the individual potatoes that are shrink wrapped in plastic? WHY??? I am not sure who is coming up with these ideas or why. It is getting harder and harder to find loose carrots, mushrooms, potatoes, green beans, apples, celery, or any produce that has no packaging or are pre-portioned in plastic bags "with a convenient carry handle." Hey, just take the produce out of the plastic carry handle bag and put it directly into your reusable bag! I've done it and the plastic police are yet to catch me. Bring your own produce bags and reuse bags that magically appear in your home for this purpose. It makes it easy for the checker if you keep different items in different bags so they can be weighed separately, but they can be final bagged together. Amazon has several washable bag options, and Sprouts has

some good ones you can buy in store. If you must use a plastic produce bag in store (happens to us all from time to time), then keep it and reuse it where possible.

2. **Bring your own reusable grocery bags and produce bags.** I keep mine stashed in my trunk, so I won't forget them at home. I prefer to buy the washable ones when possible; they easily go into the washing machine when needed and air dry quickly. I often get them for free from tradeshows and vendors (sure, I'll sport your logo for a free reusable bag!). When purchasing is necessary, you can usually find them for somewhere between $1-$5 each. Start with a couple and add to your collection as you can. Reusing plastic or paper bags from stores is another great option. I have gotten to the point of remembering them every time at the grocery store (it takes practice), but I still struggle when I go to any other kind of store. When I forget the bags in the car, I just put the loose items back into the cart and wheel it out to the car and bag them there, or carry loose items out to the car.

3. **Refuse unneeded bags.** Nothing will raise my blood pressure like watching someone carry a few items to a checkout, then put them in a bag to carry them to the car. Come on, fella—you managed to carry that all the way through the store without a bag; do you really need one to get it across the parking lot? You might want to blame self-checkouts for this, but this problem existed long before self-checkouts. Either the checkout clerk automatically puts it in a bag, or they say, "Do you want a bag?" and the default answer is yes. JUST SAY NO. I almost never use self-checkout (the why is a story for a different time), so if I don't have my

bags, I try to remember to tell the clerk I don't need a bag before we start. If I am late and they have already bagged it, I ask them to keep the bag. The silliest situation I have encountered is getting a sandwich from a chain store that has plastic bags with their logo on them and handles that fit a single sandwich in it. Not only is this unnecessary and useless, but it is also an expense that the store must bear which serves no purpose. Their logo is ALL OVER the paper the sandwich is wrapped in, so what are you gaining? Try stopping one of their employees from putting your sandwich in the bag, I dare you. No matter how many times I say it in each visit, they still put it in the bag, then when I take it out and hand them the bag back, they look at me like I'm insane. I have no idea if that bag is used again, all I can do is throw that starfish back and hope it's okay!

4. **Soaps, shampoo, and conditioner**

    a. **Laundry soap** - we have many options for laundry soap these days, including powder, liquid, tablets, strips, and probably some I have not encountered yet. I have tried just about everything. From a cleaning perspective, I have found them all to work fine, but environmentally there are some challenges. Liquids come in hard plastic containers, and tablets are wrapped in plastic that melt during the cycle and contribute to water contamination and microplastics in the environment. I have been using laundry strips for a number of years that come in a compostable box, so are considered zero waste. Laundry powders come in recyclable and compostable boxes, also, but require many boxes per year to be purchased versus one large box of laundry strips that will last nearly two years. Note: many of the high efficiency washing machines these days recommend liquid detergent. I have found that the strip detergents work just fine in these washing machines. If you find yourself with plastic containers for liquid detergent and wish to reuse them, find a local zero-waste store. These are also called refilleries or bulk refill stores. These kinds of stores have bulk supplies and will refill your existing containers with every kind of detergent and soap you can imagine. They typically offer zero-waste, plastic-free options for most any consumable in your home. Zero-waste stores are an amazing resource for finding plastic free and refill options. You can use any old container you already have, or they can sell you sturdy reusable containers. Most have an area where you can drop off unneeded clean containers that are free to anyone that needs one. One of the great things about those plastic laundry soap containers is they are very sturdy and will last for years of refills!

b. **Hand soap** – at some point in time, many of us made the switch from bar soaps to liquid soap and never looked back. For kitchen and bathroom sinks, I get it, plus for those who are avid decorators, you can buy seasonal décor containers that add to the ambiance of your home. There are two options I have exercised here. The first is to make your own liquid soap. While it is much cheaper than buying it already in liquid form, I did not find it preferable. I only tried it once, and I am glad I know how to do it, but I think it takes some practice to get it just right. The next option is to refill my larger containers at the zero-waste store and use those to fill my various containers around the house that get used year after year. Another option is to switch to bar soaps. I am a fan of artisan soaps that last much longer than commercial soap, discussed below.

c. **Shampoo, conditioner, and bar soaps**– I have been having some fun with this the last few years. Of course, I have refilled liquids at the zero-waste store numerous times, but I have also tried many bar options. Currently in my shower, you will find three bars—one for the body, one for shampoo, and one for conditioner. These are all handmade artisan bars, which I had been avoiding because of the perceived cost, but here is what I learned: it is cheaper to use these than it is to use commercial bar soap or liquid shampoo and conditioner! Not just a little cheaper, but quite a lot! Why? Because first on the ingredient list of most, if not all, of these commercial products is WATER. You pay for mostly water and a little bit of cleaning agent, some nice smells, lots of chemicals and a foaming agent. Artisan soap bars have a much higher concentration of cleaning agents and far less water. An artisan soap or hair care bar will last you at least three times longer than a bottle of liquid bodywash, commercial bar soap, shampoo or conditioner. The artisan soap is small and appears to be quite expensive, but in the long run it is better quality and will save you money. I have had a body bar that lasted nearly a year with my husband and I both using it daily. I currently have a conditioning bar that has been in use for more than six months and is showing very few signs of reduction. BONUS – you are supporting small business!

5. **Toothpaste** – You are not likely to find a plastic-free toothpaste option at a big chain store, but they are out there. I use tooth powder regularly and really like the clean-from-the-dentist feeling I get. The name of the game here is the less ingredients, the better. The tooth powder I use does not have a foaming agent (because it's not necessary), but many people prefer to have one. I had a recent incident getting through TSA with my toothpaste, so I tried tooth tablets. They are pretty fun and work well (check out my YouTube video on tooth tablets), and no one is yelling "SECURITY!" Various options are available at your local zero-waste store or on Amazon.

6. **Deodorant** is another thing you are not likely to find in a plastic-free option at a chain store, but again Amazon and your local zero-waste store are here to rescue you. Use cream deodorant in a glass container and refill it. It is available in various scents or unscented if you prefer, and aluminum-free deodorant is best for your health.

7. **Flatware** – When I say flatware, I mean utensils – knives, forks, spoons, and chopsticks, if you are more coordinated than I am. I have been on a campaign to ditch single-use flatware since I was in college, where I saw the unbelievable amount of waste that was happening on campus. I wrote a proposal to my campus to ditch the single-use flatware, and it was adopted some years later. That makes me feel like the little girl on the beach tossing the starfish back in the water – I made a difference for at least some of them! With a bit of

effort, it isn't really that hard to ditch plastic flatware in your life. It's a lot like when you start needing reading glasses—you just have to put them everywhere, so they are nearby when you need them! I carry flatware with me in my purse, backpack, and in my car to avoid using disposables. Much like just saying no to bags you don't need at the grocery store, just say no to plastic flatware when you are out and about or picking up takeout. I have never understood why the default of so many businesses is to give you plastic utensils when you are getting takeout—are that many people sitting in their car and eating their food? Don't most people take it home where they presumably already have utensils? I have often considered offering my sustainability consulting services to stores and restaurants that do these silly wasteful, expensive things. I wonder if they would hire me! You can get reusable portable options in their own carry case on Amazon and in zero-waste stores. We will talk more about how to eliminate disposable flatware at parties and gatherings in chapter eleven.

Food storage containers - avoid using plastic containers for food storage. I admit I jumped straight on the plastic container bandwagon when these came out. With all the family gatherings we do, these were the best when sending people home with leftovers, because there was no need to worry so much about getting the containers back later. Most households have that cabinet where you'll I find plastic containers of every shape, size, and brand ... with a plethora of mismatched lids that cannot be explained. Every year or so, you must go through them all, tossing most of them in the trash or recycle bin, only to start over again. In addition to the waste, when food is heated in plastic containers, the chemicals from the plastics leach into our food and can cause health problems. No good! I have personally started switching over to glass containers, solving the waste problem, as well as the concern over chemicals, but I will use the plastics until they can be used no more.

I often hear the argument that reducing the use of plastics is not needed because they are recyclable. It is important to remember that just because something CAN be recycled does not mean that it will be. There are several considerations:

1. The availability of recycling and the ability to recycle various types of plastic vary greatly depending on your local area. Having lived in several different states and having researched the availability of recycling in areas where I travel, it is astonishing the variation of availability, access, and rules for recycling. Some areas have no availability for trash pickup, let alone recycling. Other areas have curbside recycling available to residents, while 10 miles away in another municipality, it is not available.

2. Not all plastics are recyclable, either because it is not available in that area or because it contains a mix of plastics that have different properties, and the technology is not available.

3. The production of plastic uses many toxic chemicals.

4. Production and recycling of plastic consumes a large amount of energy and water.

5. Transportation produces pollution and greenhouse gas emissions.

6. No plastics are compostable. As a matter of fact, since mass use of plastics is only 50 years old, we still don't know if plastics will ever break down and if they can decompose,

how long it will take. Some suggest that the number could be as high as tens of thousands of years! I have recently conducted some experiments with plastics that claim to be compostable. Six months later, they are intact in my compost bins, so I am calling mule fritters on these claims. Even if they did degrade, what are they leaving behind?

7. Studies have shown that less than 20% of plastics produced are recycled, and many studies show numbers closer to 10%. The rest of it ends up in landfills or in the ocean!

Therefore, I'm an advocate for creating awareness and encouraging a reduction in plastic usage, even if it is in the smallest of ways. The good news is every one of you can make a difference by reducing plastics in your daily life, simply choosing to buy a version of the product you need that does not come in a plastic container, and replacing useful items like water bottles and flatware with ones that are sturdy and can be reused thousands of times, instead of once or only a few times. It can be that simple! You don't have to make radical changes to your life to throw a few of your own starfish back into the ocean. Changing one, two, or a few things, you can reduce plastic waste and contamination.

Some retailers have jumped on the plastic-free bandwagon, as well. Nike recently implemented Move to Zero, a program designed for the retailer to achieve zero carbon and zero waste by the year 2025. In a recent shopping trip, I noticed a sign in their establishment, stating that they will not provide shopping bags unless the customer requests one. I was excited to see this!! Unfortunately, the implementation of this is not what it should be, I had to remind the clerk I didn't need a bag when they automatically put my purchase in one. (Might be another consulting opportunity here!

Announcement of change is not the same as implementation of change!) Other stores have made similar moves. Aldi stores achieved their goal of removing all plastic bags at checkouts in 2023. Stores that followed suit include Ikea, Adidas, Costco, Sam's Club, and Whole Foods. I believe that with awareness, that policy will spread to many stores across the country. I would like to pause here and address "single-use bags" for stores and areas that have implemented this policy. At the time of this writing, they are still offering plastic bags, but they are considered "reusable" because they are made of thicker plastic. This is like saying you are going to solve world hunger by going on a hunger strike. This does nothing to address the problem of plastic bags in the environment or change people's habits, much like charging ten cents a bag does very little, if anything, to deter people from taking them. The only solution here is to avoid taking them in the first place. If you are like me and somehow end up with some anyway (I believe this is related to the socks that disappear in the dryer – I have less socks but more plastic bags. I have not decoded this one yet, but I am sure it's related…), reuse them until they fall apart, then recycle them. Many grocery stores have a recycle bin in front of the store specifically for grocery and produce bags.

It all starts with awareness, which leads to a change in habits. Whether you adopt several plastic-free measures or just one, you are making a positive impact, saving one starfish at a time and breaking up with plastic.

"Hey, Dee!"

Commonly-asked Questions

1. Hey, Dee: I don't like the metallic taste that sometimes comes from metal water bottles. What are other sustainable options?

   My water bottle is made of aluminum, it's lighter and does not have that metallic taste you mention. The aluminum does attach to the minerals in the water, so you have to give it a good scrub now and then. A plastic reusable is also fine and should last you many years. Ideally, a plastic one would be recyclable at the end of its usable life.

2. Hey, Dee: I can't find a refillery in my area; what can I do?

   Buy in large quantities to the best of your ability to reduce overall packaging. When possible, choose options that don't have plastic packaging. Choose items in solid form instead of liquid, such as shampoo and conditioning bars, soap bars, laundry sheets or powder.

3. Hey, Dee: There are no zero-waste stores near me; what can I do?

   The Internet can be your friend here! There are many Facebook groups and Internet sites (including Amazon) that provide options and resources for reducing waste with zero-waste products. Do your homework, and don't buy something just because it says it's eco-friendly, green, or sustainable. Claiming this with no evidence of it being true is called green washing. Ask yourself how it is sustainable, and critically look at the product and its packaging before choosing.

4. Hey, Dee: How can I provide my kids with more sustainable toys?

   I am so glad you asked! Many kids' items these days are made of cheap plastic and have a lifespan of minutes to hours. There are stores that are dedicated to eco-friendly, educational and non-toxic kids toys and clothes. Bonus – these items last much longer than the cheap ones! My favorite spot is Marley and Moose (marleyandmoose.com) for high-quality toys and clothes and supplies for littles, including nursery items. They have an online store and fabulous customer service.

5. Hey, Dee: I am concerned about how my family will react to all these changes. How should I handle this?

Slowly, and a little deviously! I am loading you up on options and choices but do not forget that you don't have to do it all at once. In fact, I would say be careful and deliberate about how you proceed. Start small, take some time and let everyone adjust (or see if they notice). I tend to ask for forgiveness rather than permission when I start a new thing, and it has worked well for me. There is a natural human tendency to resist change, so sometimes talking about it up front is self-defeating, and you will get stopped before you even start. I was amazed how many times I made changes, particularly in my purchasing habits, and the family appeared to be oblivious. No one noticed when I slowly transitioned to cooking all our meals dairy free, then gluten free, including the big holiday meals. What reaction do you think I would have gotten if I told them in advance? It's really quite fun to let the cat out of the bag once in a while when I tell them they have been eating it that way for years. My sister who was scorning my dairy-free ice cream last week polished off a container last night with delight!

Avoid, Reuse, Repurpose, Compost, Recycle, Landfill

4 What the Fuzz? Low Hanging Fruit!

I want to share with you one of my favorite stories of my decades-long attempt to live in concert with nature, even when nature had her own ideas. You will hear me say often, we are not in control, mother nature is, and I get frequent reminders of this life lesson.

In 2010, my husband and I were finally able to make a move we had been anticipating for a while—out of a neighborhood and into a home with acreage, in the same rural town where we had been living. We each had our laundry list of requirements, land for me and an up-to-date house for him. I was finally back to my roots—an environment where we have space for the animals to roam, no city lights, and quiet. This house gave me lots of room to experiment, and many of the adventures in this book were born. We also got a few things that we were not expecting.

When we moved in toward the end of summer, there was virtually no landscaping around the house. It was rather barren, except for a few scraggly bushes that had no irrigation. This was understandable, given that the house had been empty for a while—the housing market had taken a dive a couple of years earlier. Naturally, nothing had been maintained or cared for. For the most part, anything that was there was left to its own devices and ultimately became the product of nature. While I'm no stranger to neglected plants and nursing them back to health, there was a strange plant that looked more like a large bush that was bearing fruit. The fruit was greenish and had fuzz like a peach, but that seemed odd to me because I know peaches grow on trees, not bushes. I love fruit and will most any kind, but peaches are not in my top ten; I prefer the similar, but firmer, cousin—the nectarine.

Since this was a living plant and it produced some kind of fruit, I wanted to save it. I watered the tree and watched the fruit grow and turn color, waiting for them to soften as peaches do, indicating they are ripe. I kept checking and checking, but to my bewilderment, they remained firm. I decided to take one into the house and cut it open. When I did, I couldn't believe my eyes—under that fuzzy skin was a nectarine. A nectarine belongs to the same genome as a peach, but it has a recessive gene for smooth skin, a firmer texture, and a slightly different taste. I didn't have peaches, after all, but I also didn't really have nectarines. What I had was a hybrid fruit—I had fuzzy nectarines!

I really wanted to understand how this happened and wished I still had my grandfather to ask. He had been a professional grove manager, and an avid fruit free extraordinaire and master gardener. When I was a kid, my grandfather grafted a lemon and a lime together, and he gave me a tree, which produced limons—a yellow-green fruit that tasted like a bit of each.

I summoned the spirit of my grandfather and called my friend who had been raised on a peach farm, hoping for answers. After looking at some photos, he said, "Oh, what you have here is a grafted tree that wasn't done properly." There may be many of you out there that know a lot more about this than I did, but I am still a complete novice, and I had a lot of questions.

A properly grafted tree uses the base of one tree (such as a peach) and grafts on a twig of another fruit (such as a nectarine). The object is to get a hybrid fruit; this is how you end up with things like plumcots (a plum and an apricot) and grapefruit (pomelo and orange). The graft worked in one respect—I got a hybrid fruit, but the tree ended up more like a large bush.

Sharing with Wildlife

The mystery was solved, but I was posed with another challenge—it seemed that the wildlife likes fuzzy nectarines, too! The fruit was low enough to the ground that the deer were able to reach most of it. You know, those deer didn't even wait until it was ripe! I would come out some mornings, and there would be hundreds of pits on the ground and the fruit was completely green. The birds were not much better; once the fruit started blushing, the birds would take a bite or two out of most of the fruit long before it was fully ripe. In many areas, squirrels are also a frequent fruit thief. I don't mind sharing, but nature doesn't particularly care if they leave anything for me, so I started thinking about how I could protect some of the fruit without posing any danger to the local wildlife.

I was able to (kind of) net the tree/bush when it was smaller. It was quite a sight – all five feet of me trying to toss a net over a big bushy thing. I couldn't use a ladder because there were things in the way and the plant is on a hillside. It was fun to imagine my neighbors watching me fight with the net, getting it caught in the breeze and netting myself or caught in the branches. I doubt anyone noticed, but I had fun cracking myself up in the meantime. I have been pruning the lower growth for years now, encouraging it to grow up like a tree so netting is out of the question unless I can get Shaquille O'Neal to come over and help me. Wouldn't THAT be cool??

Here are species-specific tips and tricks for natural deterrents that won't hurt you, your food, or the critters:

- Birds - My grandfather used those little, tiny pie tins on string tied into the tree to keep the birds away. Any reflective object will help with birds—I have even heard of people using wind chimes.

- Deer - high fencing at least 8' tall (remember, they are good jumpers), or companion planting with lavender and marigolds near the fruit trees. Electric fences are also an option for an effective deterrent. It won't hurt them, but they are smart enough to move along for an easier target. Electric fences should be placed a few feet from the edge of the tree canopy and about 3' off the ground.

- Squirrels – are the toughest little critters to deter, in my opinion. They are fast, smart, and have thumbs—maybe not as good as ours, but still! Humane trap and remove is the most effective long-term method (see chapter five for more on that). Motion-activated sprinklers, ultrasonic devices, garlic and pepper sprays are somewhat effective and can be made at home. They are excellent climbers, so if you choose fencing, it must be more than 4' tall and have nothing they can grab onto to climb. Tree guards wrapped around the trunk to make climbing difficult can help, as well as netting.

> Lastly, predator urine can be purchased online or in gardening stores and spread around the base of the tree.

- Location - Be cognizant of where you are planting your trees, and make sure you are not planting near things that attract deer and squirrels, like a stream, salt lick, or feeder.

Assuming you can save enough of the harvest for you to use, you can very well end up with far more than you need. We get many pounds of fresh fruit from the fuzzy nectarine each year that we share with our friends and neighbors. You can also do some canning or freezing (preserving food will be discussed in chapter twelve).

One year, it produced so much fruit, but the fruit would not ripen. I called my fruit friend, and again he saved the day. "You need to thin it," he said.

He explained that I needed to pick the smaller fruit off to allow the larger fruit to finish maturing. In other words, the tree had only so much energy to give, and the fruit needed more space to finish growing. It worked like a charm. It feels a little strange pinching off fruit and throwing it to the ground – I feel a little like I am robbing my tree of her young, but it is necessary to get a better harvest. I have had to do the same for enthusiastic tomato plants.

Planting fruit-bearing trees and plants is one of the best ways to become more sustainable. A single fruit-bearing tree can often provide more than the family needs of that fruit. You can preserve the excess (see chapter twelve), share with friends and neighbors, or barter the fruit for things you need.

Whatever your garden grows and however you choose to preserve it, your garden, bushes, trees, and land can become a self-sustaining food source that will provide you with nature's best unprocessed foods. It takes just a little time and effort to give your plants and trees the best growing conditions, and they will reward you for years to come. Be sure you consult a growing guide for your area to ensure you are selecting plants that will do well in your area (see chapter twelve for more information) so you have the best chance for success and utilize plants appropriate for the climate.

I'll never know if the person that grafted the tree intended to create a fuzzy nectarine it or if it was an accident of some kind, but I view it as a gift. They say when life gives you lemons, make lemonade. Well, life gave me fuzzy nectarines, and I'm using them to live a more sustainable life!

The Accidental Landscaper

I never intended to become a landscaper but become one I did for our un-landscaped home. When we moved into this new country home, it was at the same time beautiful and not much to look at. I think a real estate agent would say it had "potential." The house itself was quite large by our standards and only about nine years old but had been alternately cared for and not cared for in its lifetime. Based on discussions with the neighbors, the people who built the house took great care of it, but the most recent owners did not. Trash had been dumped in a drainage ditch at the front part of the property, and my husband spent months cleaning it out. Apparently, the previous owners were fond of goat meat as we found numerous goat carcasses semi buried in various places on the property. Upon finding these, my husband was a bit alarmed. To say the least, you find some strange things when cleaning up large properties, I leave that to my husband, and I work with the living things!

My grandmother taught me how to plant and keep roses, so I have had roses at every house I have ever had in my adult life. When we moved in, there were four struggling scraggly rose bushes in the front of the house, so I set about saving them along with the fuzzy nectarine. There was much planting to be done at the front of the house to make it look lived in and welcoming, but I quickly realized what I was in for. The soil on this property was rock with a little dirt in it. I'm not kidding; you need power tools to plant anything. Fortunately, I have a jackhammer, and I'm not afraid to use it. Now, for anyone who knows me, this is simultaneously not surprising and hilarious. I am 5 feet, 0 inches tall. That's right – a flat 60" until I put my work boots on—then I am 61". I'm no longer the twig I was in my youth, but suffice it to say I am not a large person. I spent over 100 hours jackhammering in various places around our house to plant things that may or may not grow, and I am proud of every single one of my survivors. So, soil conditions are a challenge I was going to have to learn to deal with.

Then there was the local wildlife. To help set the scene, this property is in the Southern California mountains a bit and is up against a national forest. In Southern CA terms, that means a lot of open space, but not pine trees, more like brush and some oak trees. It is a little over four acres with intermittent fencing. We have never completed fencing because we like to see the wildlife wander through the property and leave things in their natural state as much as possible. We see roadrunners, bobcats, coyotes, deer, rabbits, squirrels, and many other beautiful animals. However, the free roaming wildlife presents challenges for landscaping. Deer and rabbits absolutely love to eat plants, especially newly planted ones. I was raised in the country and had gardens and fruit trees, but I never had much trouble with critters eating my plants. The difference is fencing and dogs, plain and simple. My parents' property was fenced, and we always had a couple dogs running around outside. Without dogs and fences, you get lots of hungry rabbits and deer lining up for your landscaping buffet.

I went to the local nursery to select plants that look good and are drought tolerant. If the tag said something like "okay in rocky soil," it was even better. Mind you, I had no real plan beyond the five or six plants I was choosing in the moment (five to six seemed to be how many holes I could jackhammer in a day). I wasn't then and still am not great at plant names; I was going by two things: what I thought looked good and what I had seen in drought-tolerant plantings in other places. I excitedly made my purchases and went home to plant them, careful to amend the soil and water them as I planted. At first, things went well, and I checked on my new plantings daily to make sure they looked happy. By the second round of planting, the rabbits knew something was up and came up to investigate while we innocently slept on the other side of the wall. I woke up one morning, grabbed my cup of coffee, and walked out front to check on my new plants—that were now nubs. Those cute little fuzzy marauders ate my new plants down to a nub and didn't even leave a thank you note!

If I can manage to get the tasty plants out of their infancy, the rabbits seem to leave them alone. So, my next step was rabbit wire cages around the tastier plants. It should work, right? Rabbit wire to keep the rabbits out makes sense. I did this around six or eight of my specimens. In a couple of days, I noticed nibble marks on the leaves— what the…? It took me a while to figure it out, but rabbits come in different sizes – the small ones could still wiggle through. I was starting to channel Elmer Fudd at this point—why you rascally rabbits! I considered for a moment getting my shotgun, but no, this was not the answer—we must live in concert with nature, I reminded myself. So back to Home Depot I went for chicken wire. Let's see those rascally rabbits get through that! Chicken wire did the trick.

Planting for aesthetics not only beautifies your space, but it can support local wildlife with pollen, shelter, and nesting spots. Choosing diverse flowering plants will add beauty and support the biodiversity of your local area. Now that I am a more experienced landscaper, the experimental landscaping done at the Southern California home is planned to be completely redone in the next couple of years. It will transition to perennial flowers to support pollinators and food-bearing plants in raised beds so we can avoid all the jackhammering. The beds will be tall to help keep the rabbits out, but I might still have to contend with the deer and squirrels. I wish I had thought of this years ago, but the accidental landscaping was a wonderful learning experience for me. I have had the additional experience of moving to Northern Colorado and learning to landscape and garden there, which is a whole different skill set with different challenges.

The takeaway is that you don't have to know everything—in fact, you don't have to know much at all. Start with a few plants and see what happens. Then plant a few more, and a few more. Plant a tree, shrub, bush, or flower. All plants do the heavy lifting of exchanging carbon dioxide for oxygen and creating a healthy, breathable environment for humans and animals, but they also add beauty, biodiversity, and environments for all kinds of wildlife, bees, and deer alike.

"Hey, Dee!"

Commonly-asked Questions

1. Hey, Dee: I have never gardened before; how do I know how much to water and where to plant things?

   This is a question every beginner has. Look, you will make mistakes, and nature will set you straight. The best way to start is to do a little bit of online research for your planting zone. Look up "US planting zone by zip code" and put your zip code in. Once you know your planting zone, you can research plants and trees that are appropriate for your zone. Please note that nurseries and garden stores DO sell things that are not appropriate for your zone! Each plant type you buy will have a tag that tells you how much sun it needs; sometimes they tell you about watering, and sometimes you have to look that up separately. What will your local wildlife eat before it's 24 hours old? That is another story and takes some trial and error.

2. Hey, Dee: I live in a situation where I can't plant things outside. What can I do?

   Plant indoors! I have many indoor plants that beautify my space. Learning to manage indoor plants is a different skill set than managing outdoor plants, and I came into it much later in my experiments. Succulents are a great place to start; snake plants and creeping charley are easy care and maintenance.

3. Hey, Dee: Every time I have plants inside, I end up with little bugs flying around. How can I prevent that from happening without using chemicals?

   This is one that took me a while and quite a few tries to manage. One method is to spread diatomaceous earth in the soil of the plant. It's basically crushed up shells, and although it appears to have the consistency of baby powder to us, it's like tiny razor blades to flying and crawling insects. This works well inside and outside for anything that crawls. This is effective but takes some time and re-application. The second thing I did inside was add a carnivorous plant. I chose an octopus plant for my house, and it works very well! They need to stay moist to be happy, so it is currently my highest maintenance plant, but it gives me beautiful little flowers a couple times a year to add to the beauty of my indoor garden.

Avoid, Reuse, Repurpose, Compost, Recycle, Landfill

5 ...SQUIRREL!

While all insects and animals are part of the food chain and our environment, there are some that can proudly claim the title of "pest," meaning they are an unwelcome nuisance. Even worse are those pests that destroy our gardens and native plants, wreaking havoc on our food sources and becoming the backyard bullies that everyone wishes would go away. The adorable delinquents that immediately come to mind are squirrels and racoons, but there are many more insects and mammals that can fall into this category.

Our property in Southern California attracts various pests, including ants, spiders, mice, rats, coyotes, grasshoppers, squirrels, rabbits, deer, gophers, and racoons. Some are visitors, seeking a bite to eat or temporary lodging as they pass through on their way to their ultimate destination, while others establish themselves as squatters and settle down to raise generations of their families and mooch off our land. Their populations grow, and with the power of their numbers, they chase everything else, including our sanity, out of their territory.

On that note, whoever coined the phrase "multiply like rabbits" has never met their nemesis: the squirrel.

Since we always had dogs running around, we never had a squirrel problem at my parents' property and did not have them when we lived in town, either. So, we found yet another topic that I was unfamiliar with and learned by the seat of my pants. Not being familiar with squirrels of any kind, Southern California has ground squirrels and Colorado has tree squirrels, I used to think they were cute and harmless. In the beginning, we watched them from afar as they scampered along, chasing each other's bushy little tails. We didn't have a squirrel problem back then, but our neighbors had plenty of them. They had horses, and the steady diet of alfalfa and grain appealed to the squirrel population, keeping them so fat and happy that they didn't want to leave—that is until those neighbors moved, taking their horses and the source of squirrel treats along with them. No longer having access to a free 24-hour buffet, the squirrels packed their bags and went in search of a new address. They needed to only go a few football fields away before they found a spot they liked, which just so happened to be near the end of our long driveway. This location is along our tiny little road and near the driveways of several properties. I thought they had settled here, but it turns out this was just their temporary command post while they planned a full-frontal assault on our and our neighbors' properties.

I'd heard horror stories about them knocking over trash bins, destroying compost piles and gardens, and taking over bird feeders. It seems they were calling in some reinforcements, as their numbers kept increasing. It became apparent that I wasn't dealing with a few squirrels, but an entire regiment. Squirrels are survivors, rapid multipliers, expert evaders, and master excavators, digging underground tunnels that provide them with multiple hideaways and escape routes that make it more than difficult to root them out. I knew if I didn't start fighting back immediately, I would be overrun by the enemy.

Before long, their front line began moving up the driveway. I set out on a search for natural squirrel control methods, but that search for solutions fell short. The bad news is there isn't much available short of having a platoon of dogs and cats to keep them harassed … or a squirrel gun and a dead eye. I already had cats, both feral and tame, so I knew that alone wasn't enough. Realizing that there was no way I was going to get them to wave their white flag and retreat, I devised my own battle plan. I had to kill the squirrels, which was the humane thing to do since injuring them would cause them to suffer. If they were dead, at least they would become part of the food chain for many of the hungry animals that passed through, and their numbers would be curbed.

Armed with a pellet gun and the proper loads (yes, there is a proper load to kill a squirrel), I felt a bit like a hick, knowing what I must have looked like walking around with a weapon while mumbling gibberish about a bunch of squirrels. Thankfully, no one called the sheriff—that I know of, anyway. The bad news is that those little suckers are really, really fast. It requires a lot of patience to sit and wait for them to pop their cute little heads out of a hole and start running, only to dive at lightning speed into yet another nearby hole. Now, I am a pretty good shot, but I didn't hit a single squirrel. I think I scared the fur off a few, but I walked away with no kills on my first day out. The next weekend, I tried again … and again got the same results. I hadn't shot a single squirrel; however, after several weekend raids on their population, I noticed I was seeing fewer of them. Huh? How could that be? Did they retreat back to headquarters to devise a new attack, or was I harassing them so much they decided to surrender? If so, GREAT! Mission accomplished, but still, that seemed too easy.

Fast forward another couple of weeks, I was talking with one of my neighbors about the invasion and mysterious retreat of the squirrels. I noticed a gleam in his eye as a knowing smile spread across his face, and I knew I was missing something. "What?" I prodded. "What happened to the squirrels?"

He chuckled and said, "Well, I'm not sure everyone would appreciate what I did." He went on to explain that he'd been trapping the squirrels and relocating them to an open area nearby. That seemed like the perfect solution—the squirrels were free from harm and no longer a menace to us! However, there was just one little problem—anytime you trap and release, you are increasing the population of that species in another area and effectively introducing a menace that did not exist before or increasing a menace that was already there. The open space he was releasing them into had homes nearby, and one of the homeowners approached him in the act, asking that he find another place to take the squirrels as their neighborhood was now invaded by the little rascals. He hadn't taken care of the problem; instead, he'd moved it to another area.

I did not think of the trapping and relocation and might have tried the same thing if I had, but in the end my neighbor came to the same conclusion that I had—our only viable option was to shoot the squirrels and leave them for the local wildlife. Unsure of my reaction, his face became flushed when he told me this, and he refused to meet my eye. Any fear that I wouldn't approve was eliminated altogether when I offered to lend him my gun and some of my squirrel loads. It was the least I could do, knowing that he's obviously a more practiced shot than I am!

While there is some humor in the saga of Dee and the disappearing squirrels, I am aware that there are some who will take exception to the pest control method we took. I get that. I love animals of all kinds, too, and I was taught to NEVER, EVER let an animal suffer. I can go into some gory childhood stories about how seriously my parents took that, but I will spare you those stories here. Suffice it to say that although I don't want all animals for pets, and my furry little pets do have their special place in my world, I don't believe in killing anything unless it's necessary, and when it is, make sure that the animal is safe to become part of the food chain (no poisons). I would never want any kind of animal—including humans as we are animals, too—to suffer at my hands or yours. In the case of squirrels and other invasive pests, there is a delicate balance between their survival and their contribution to the demise of other species in the animal kingdom. It is when that balance is jeopardized that extreme measures can be justified.

The first course of pest control is prevention, and I'm an advocate for allowing the natural order of the food chain to do its job. However, there are times when pests are dangerous, unhealthy, or out of control, and that is when I encourage natural, non-toxic deterrents that will have minimal to no impact on the air, land, water, and the other living species that share our planet.

Tree Squirrels, Voles, and Prairie Dogs, oh my!

Before we moved to Colorado, I spent some time there for work. I had signed on for an eight-month contract to oversee the design of a new manufacturing plant and had never been to Colorado before. I was immediately taken by the vast open space (compared to Southern California) and the beauty of the mountains. As my eight-month contract turned into a three-year contract to include overseeing the construction, living in a hotel was no longer desirable, so my husband and I decided to purchase a townhouse. I quickly fell in love with this beautiful state!

With a new area comes new critters. Here I met tree squirrels, voles, and prairie dogs. Living in a townhouse and having no yard or garden to maintain, I just watched the squirrels perform their daily acrobatics, running along fence tops, jumping from tree to tree, and chasing one another.

Much like their California cousins, they are crafty survivors, plentiful, and very destructive. You remember how I told you that the ground on our property in Southern California was so hard you needed a jackhammer to plant anything, then I told you the ground squirrels dug a tunnel network? They use their claws where we need jackhammers—that is how powerful these little fuzzballs are! In Colorado, where cold winters happen, tree squirrels can damage more than your garden; they will dig holes into the roof or sides of your house to gain access to the inside for winter. In warmer months, they are happy to live in the trees, but in winter when it's cold and the trees lose their leaves, they look for shelter, preferably in your house. Attics are a popular choice for squirrels and racoons alike. Squirrel control is a mixed bag in Colorado, especially if you live in a neighborhood. One house will have a squirrel feeder, and next door there will be squirrel traps. I am sure that those neighbors have some interesting debates.

While I was serving on the board of directors for the townhouse we bought, we were having some serious problems with squirrels and racoons digging holes in the roof and/or siding to get into the attics to nest. Being an HOA board, we had no choice but to follow local law in that area for pest control, and that meant trapping and relocating, then repairing the damage. It was time-consuming and expensive since we had to hire it out. Many of our residents have security cameras and video doorbells, like so many of us do these days. I was sent a video of a woman pulling into one of our parking areas, opening the back hatch of her car and out flew squirrels, presumably from a humane trap she had in the back of her car. While we were trapping and relocating to manage our problem, someone else was doing the same and relocating their squirrels onto our property. You are starting to see why I am not such a fan of relocation. I guess no one wants to take them on a field trip to the mountains before opening the cage. I have no idea where the pest control companies relocate them; hopefully, they are not transferring the problem to another neighborhood, although that would be a good business strategy…

Voles are like gophers and moles in that they live underground and will dig a vast tunnel network, but they are not related. Voles are rodents and look a lot like mice. Though they prefer plants, they will eat just about anything. They seem to enjoy digging their shallow tunnels in lawns, munching on grass blades and stems of the grass. (Moles will dig deeper and leave mounds of dirt at the entry/exit points.) Voles will also take up residence in your garden, partially eating root vegetables or flower bulbs.

Managing voles naturally is very similar to managing mice or rats, peanut-butter-baited snap traps will do the trick. You can also use predator urine, but it must be reapplied after rain or snow. As with all rodents, dogs, cats, owls, and snakes are the best deterrent; let the food chain work for you.

Prairie dogs, or as I call them "squeaky toys," are part of the squirrel family. The sound they make as a warning when you get near sounds just like a dog's squeaky toy to me, so it's the first thing I think of when referring to a prairie dog. They are plains-dwelling squirrels that are actually pretty cute. They don't have a long bushy tail like their tree dwelling cousins, but rather a stubby little tail. They are often seen standing outside the big mounds they leave, on their hind legs looking for danger and munching away on grass. For many, this sight may suggest a meerkat, and although there are many similarities in their family and social behaviors, they are not related. When you see them in the plains of the United States, you will see a bunch of dirt mounds that represent their elaborate underground colony, called a prairie dog town. Like many small mammals, they are not only cute but smart and complicated. Their vocabulary is one of the most advanced animal languages that have been decoded. It may be tempting to keep one as a pet, but this is not advisable. Prairie dogs and many other small mammal colonies still become infected with the bubonic plague, and it can wipe out entire prairie dog towns, as well as transfer to humans.

Natural pest control methods for prairie dogs should, of course, involve natural predators such as snakes, hawks, owls, dogs, and cats, and even ferrets. Since prairie dogs prefer wide open spaces with clear views to help them identify predators, simply putting visual obstructions up, like fences or hay bales, can deter them from colonizing an area. You can also flood their tunnel with water to discourage them from staying. Prairie dogs eat plants, but they don't much care for garlic, mint, or castor beans—planting these will act as a deterrent.

Prairie dogs have an excellent sense of smell as a protection device, so predator urine, strong smelling items like cayenne pepper, cinnamon, hot pepper flakes, white vinegar, and peppermint oil around the holes or in areas you don't want them to colonize can be effective.

"Hey, Dee!"

Commonly-asked Questions

1. Hey, Dee: I really don't want to kill any animals. What can I do?

    I get it, extreme measures aren't for everyone. Deterring the pest should always be your first stop, and to deter the pest, you must understand it. Do a little research and understand what they like to eat, where they like to live, and what in your environment might attract them, and what or who might repel them. There are many natural ways to deter a pest, sometimes it is as simple as taking away the thing they are seeking or adding something they don't like. The food chain is a wonderful thing when it's allowed to work properly, and that means making a home for some things, while discouraging others.

2. Hey, Dee: There is so much information out there about natural deterrents like homemade pepper sprays and vinegar solutions. How do I know what will work?

    Experimentation is the fun part, and sometimes it is the frustrating part. What works for me may not work for you, so you should be open to trying a few things. One thing I have noticed is that many recommendations out there are for a diluted version of cayenne pepper, peppermint oil, or whatever. If you have an immediate issue, I say start with full strength to get the issue under control, then start playing with dilutions. (Note: if you are putting something on plants, full strength could hurt or kill the plant you are trying to save. I would only do full strength on the ground.)

3. Hey, Dee: I see all kinds of commercial products out there that have labels that use words like "green, eco-friendly, safe, all-natural" and similar things that lead us to believe they are environmentally safe and natural. Are they?

   One of the things that we get hit with a lot in the sustainability world is something called green washing. What that means is that words are used for marketing purposes that don't have any defined legal meaning to lead the consumer to believe that their product is safe, non-toxic, or environmentally responsible. It is important to understand that these words have no legal definition, so they can be used freely. That often means they are meaningless and, therefore, cannot be trusted when we are searching for the truth. With any packaged item, first look at the ingredients. If you see any chemical names or indecipherable words, I urge you to put it down and move on. If you see a list of things like cayenne pepper, garlic, and vinegar, ask yourself if it makes sense for you to purchase this item or give your DIY skills a try and make it yourself.

   I want to take a moment to address that the same thing happens with food labeling. The words "all natural" or "natural" have no legal definition. The FDA has looked into this, and there have been a number of lawsuits. "The FDA has considered the term natural to mean that nothing artificial or synthetic (including all color additives regardless of source) has been included in, or has been added to, a food that would not normally be expected to be in that food." This does not address food production, pesticides, manufacturing methods, or processing. It also does not consider whether or not the item has any nutritional or health benefit. Caveat emptor, indeed!

Avoid, Reuse, Repurpose, Compost, Recycle, Landfill

6 START BUGGING YOUR BUGS!

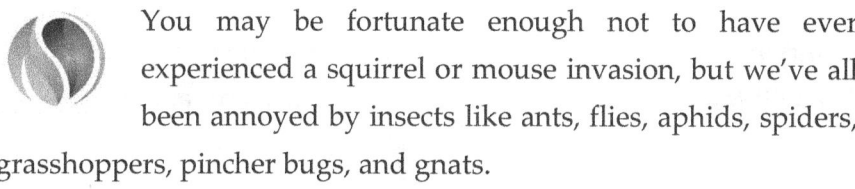

You may be fortunate enough not to have ever experienced a squirrel or mouse invasion, but we've all been annoyed by insects like ants, flies, aphids, spiders, grasshoppers, pincher bugs, and gnats.

Ants in My Plants

There are more than 10,000 known ant species in the world; it is believed there are about twenty quadrillion ants alive on the planet at any time according to a study done by the University of Western Australia (that is 15 zeroes after the 20, in case you were wondering!) Ants are incredible little dynamos that can carry more than three times their own weight. They are a vital part of our ecosystem and really fun to just sit and watch if you have a few extra minutes. They have a complex social system and are the very definition of hard workers. Much like bees, they have a queen and workers that have various jobs, such as foraging, larvae care, and soldiers for defense of the nest. What do they do for us, you ask? They aerate the soil, allowing oxygen and water to penetrate the layers aiding in plant growth, disperse seeds, add nutrients to the soil with their waste, and redistribute nutrients in the soil. They are also a vast food source for many other animals.

Ants are mother nature's garbage women, breaking down organic matter that is dead and decaying and bringing it back to the nest for consumption. I say garbage women because the foragers are sterile females, not males. The women are doing the heavy lifting! They are bringing home the bacon and frying it up in the pan! The women are having the babies, caring for the babies, getting the food! Wait, what are the males doing again? No, they are not sitting on the sofa watching the game; their job is defending the nest and breeding. They probably like beer, though.

Plants and ants are symbiotic, helping each other survive and thrive. We will talk more about aphids shortly, but many ant species will kill and eat aphids.

Despite how wonderful ants are, and how vital to our ecosystem, they sometimes like to hang out in large numbers in places we don't want them. They come in various colors and sizes, but their peskiness tends to be seasonal. In colder climates, they disappear in the fall and don't make an appearance again until spring when the weather warms up. In Southern California, it can be as warm in December as it is in June, so ant season is longer. The conga line usually starts at the palm tree and winds around the pool, making their way across the deck to a large planter. Conga lines of festive ants is all it takes to wreck a good outdoor gathering or barbeque, especially if you are like my friend, Kimmy, who is a bit of a pied piper of ants, and they follow her wherever she is on the patio. If we could just get them to follow her away from the area…

When we are ready to reduce the number of ants in an area, we have countless options. One only needs to take a walk through the gardening or pest control aisles of a big box store to see that there is no shortage of products, sprays, powders, and contraptions to get rid of these uninvited pests who want to crash your party.

I'm sure many of those products are effective, but I'm always cognizant of the effect that pest control products and deterrents have on people, animals, plants, and the environment. If possible, I avoid spraying anything containing chemicals around the property. At the beginning of hotter weather, I inevitably hear the conga music and know it's time to pull out the bait stations. They seem to control the ant population, and since the bait is contained, there is low risk of contaminating any other animals. This is usually all I need to do to handle the ants on my deck, the ones in the planters can stay there.

We did have an indoor incident some years ago over a particularly long and dry summer. We were getting ants often in the house, and I was employing my bleach treatment, wiping down counters and light switches with bleach daily, making sure nary a crumb was left out to attract them. (I learned the bleach trick when I lived in Texas. Seems ants don't like the strong smell, so they avoid areas that you do this in, like the kitchen.) Upstairs I go to take a shower, I turn on the shower head and about 10,000 ants came flying out. Okay, well, it's not like I counted, but it was a lot. That was it, time to call the professionals. Once upon a time, I worked for a pest control company, so I knew they had the tools to deal with this. The technician concluded we had at least one, maybe two ant colonies under the slab of our house. In this instance, I resorted to chemical means to control the infestation. I wasn't going to be showering with ants, so it had to be done, and within a couple of weeks, we were ant free. My friend Diane uses peppermint oil instead of bleach to deter ants at her house. I have to admit this would be a much less toxic option, though perhaps a little more costly. I love the smell of peppermint and will be giving it a try. Thank you for your suggestion, Diane!

Spiders Big and Small

There are over 50,000 known species of these eight-legged carnivores, and they are as important to our planet as ants and bees. Spiders are a very important part of the insect food chain that helps keep things in balance, so spiders are a welcome sight—most of the time. As long as the spiders stay outside, I leave them alone with only rare exception. Black widows are the main exception that we encounter frequently, and I do pull a spray out for that. For some reason, they particularly like the exterior slab edge of our Southern California house, where I've seen tons of them hanging out on the intricate webs they've somehow woven overnight. To keep them under control, I spray the exterior perimeter of the house twice a year, which sufficiently keeps their population at bay. Black widows tend to come out at night, so birds are not a big threat for them. I have not found any natural methods to handle the black widows; if you know of any, I would love to hear from you!

We occasionally encounter tarantulas—if you want to see me run, this is a good way to do it. For some reason, when spiders get large and hairy, I don't like them anymore. One day I came up the driveway, parked my car and a brown tarantula was right next to my car. No way I was getting out! I called my husband who was inside the house and had him put on his boots and grab a shovel to squash it. Otherwise, I wasn't coming in. Meanwhile, our cat sat there staring at me sitting in the car and could not understand why I wouldn't get out. He either didn't notice the spider or wasn't bothered by it. I know they are around, but thankfully we don't encounter them much.

Aphids

Aphids are tiny sap-sucking insects that will destroy the plants they are sucking on. They're such a nuisance that they're also known as "plant lice." Let's face it, there are some insects that you're going to get no matter what you do, and aphids are one of them. Try as you might, they're tough to get rid of entirely, but in smaller populations they are manageable. The best thing you can do is to control where they go and what they eat, using what you already know about nature. To turn their attention away from my vegetables and flowers, I provide them with a sacrificial plant that will give them what they need. This magic plant is called marigold. The aphids love the marigolds, and they don't have to look elsewhere for a food source, so they will leave my other plants alone. As a bonus, because it takes them all summer to kill a marigold, the flowers still bloom nicely and look attractive for the whole season.

Another bonus is that the marigolds attract ladybugs, which are pollinators that are beneficial to a garden and its crop, and they love to eat aphids! You see the balance here? This always reminds me of the old lady who swallowed a fly, then she swallowed a spider to catch the fly ... it's the circle of life! It is not a good idea to remove anything entirely from the ecosystem; it all has its purpose and is a food source for something else. We don't want to decimate aphids — we just want to limit their damage. Let them attract the beautiful insects that provide us with natural pest control by taking their attention off what we want to preserve and placing it on plants that'll keep them too busy to invade our entire garden. Another thing I love about marigolds is that once they're planted, I don't have to do anything more. Sometimes, I don't even have to plant them—they are perennials in zones where the winters aren't too severe, and they can reseed themselves. When the ground warms up in the spring, new plants sprout and take the place of last summer's crop.

Using marigolds as pest control extends beyond aphids; they can deter rabbits from nibbling on the tender green leaves of young plants. While I don't plant them for that purpose, I'm not surprised that it might work. Nature does provide us with plenty of plants and animals that provide a system of checks and balances to keep pest populations in control.

Ladybugs and lace wings are natural aphid predators and will help keep the populations in check. You can try attracting them with what you plant, or you can introduce them into your garden by purchasing them at your local garden center. Release them at dusk in your garden area and add them to the natural order of things.

If your winged bug army is not enough, there are other measures you can take. Dishwashing soap and water in a squirt bottle will kill aphids on contact but take care to spray your plant at a time of day when it's not in direct sunlight or you can damage the plant. Aphids prefer the new growth, especially around any new flower buds, and make sure you check the underside of leaves where they like to lay their eggs. Persistence is necessary, because the solution kills the adult aphids, but the eggs may continue to hatch. Spray every few days until all of the eggs are hatched, and you know there aren't any adult aphids left on the plant.

I discovered another natural method by accident a few years ago. Since I don't use chemical fertilizers in my garden, I started using fish emulsion as a natural fertilizer. Fish emulsion is pureed fish, and you can sure tell by the smell. It's a brown stinky liquid that is pure gold for your plants. I use a sprayer that attaches to the end of the hose and mixes the emulsion with water to spray the plants. After spraying all over my garden one year, I went back to treat some of the aphids I had seen getting a little out of control, but they were already dead! The application of the fish emulsion killed them on contact, instantly reducing their population dramatically. I had just discovered another benefit of fish emulsion!

Snatch the Pebble from My Hand, Grasshopper

You may be too young to get this reference, but if you know, you know; if you don't, you should look it up. Grasshoppers can be a pest control menace of biblical proportion under the right conditions. If the winter is warm and dry, you might be in for a battle like you have never seen before. Baby grasshoppers are so small you hardly notice them, but before long you have thousands of them eating every plant you have. Unfortunately, I haven't been as lucky in finding a way to manage the grasshopper population—other than Mother Nature. It seems the best control is a cold winter and a good hard freeze that kills off many of the eggs that were laid in the fall, reducing the number of hatchlings.

Many species of birds eat grasshoppers, some species use grasshoppers as a main food source, making up 50% of their daily diet during breeding season. Grasshoppers are fairly large insects and provide a nutritious meal for our feathered friends, and although people have a hard time catching grasshoppers, birds find it quite easy. The birds you want to attract to your yard to help control the grasshopper population are meadowlarks, harriers, cardinals, jays, crows, robin, sparrow, bluebird, starling, flycatcher, oriole, swallow, warbler, wren, blackbird, and many more. I hear chickens and turkeys love to be invited to a grasshopper buffet and can put a dent into your overpopulation problem quickly.

Another somewhat effective method is to sprinkle flour on your plants. As I understand it, the gluten sticks to their legs and builds up, eventually making it so they can't jump. *Cautionary note* – if you use this method on food crops, and you give any of it away or sell it, people with celiac disease can get sick from the wheat contamination even after the flour is washed off the plant. Since this method relies on gluten to do the dirty work, gluten-free flour won't be effective. Be aware of anyone in your life that might have celiac disease and make sure you tell them you have used this method before they become exposed.

There are some chemicals out there for grasshopper control that claim to be safe and non-toxic. Last summer, we had a biblical infestation, but I did not give in to the temptation to try them, but it was difficult. Instead, I relied on the local food chain, trimmed my clover lawn a little more often to give them a less comfortable place to hide, and trusted the system. I didn't lose any food crops, but they did damage almost every plant on the property. I am hoping for a cold wet winter, but so far, it's been warm and dry. Nature is in charge, not me!

Legalizing Weeds

What makes a weed a weed? It's simply a plant in a place we don't want it. (I remember this test question from my agriculture class in middle school, but I don't think I appreciated what it meant until much later.) Even a flower can be a weed if it's in the wrong place. The idea of weeds really came about when we started planting for aesthetics, and certain plants did not contribute to the visual impact we are seeking to achieve. When we plant things in a monoculture, a lawn for example, everything that isn't that specific type of grass stands out as different and out of place, and we then start obsessing about "weeding" to restore the monoculture. Think of a wild meadow, are there any weeds there? Not really, because it's nature's organized chaos, and we appreciate it for its wild beauty and aren't looking for a planned, organized planting. When considering what is a weed and what is not, consider the area, what is there, how that could be different, and the possibility of legalizing your weeds, or at least some of them.

Manual pulling of weeds is always the least invasive option for the environment, and that is our default. It can be time-consuming, but also very satisfying and a great opportunity to spend some time out in the sunshine. Just as it is in pest control, weed control products are plentiful. To control weeds, ingredients like vinegar, salt, borax, and soap are all safe to people, plants, and wildlife, and they are effective in preventing and eliminating weeds. It is important to note that ANYTHING you put on the soil will have some impact on it. Too much of anything that is not naturally occurring there is not good. Salty soil won't allow plant growth; the same thing happens with vinegar. Before you decide what a weed is and what must be controlled, consider this carefully. There are multiple different blends and different theories about what is effective and what is not. I haven't tried them all, but I will share one I've tried recently that has proven to do the job.

I have found 30 percent vinegar works very well to kill invasive weeds. Thirty percent vinegar can be readily purchased, put into a spray bottle and applied directly to the weed, but you only want to do this in an area that has no plantings, as it is quite strong, and it will kill all plants. I use this only in rock areas. It is a good idea to wear gloves when working with this as it can burn your skin. I've found it works well on weeds that are seemingly impossible to kill, like bindweed, which is invasive and has remarkably long roots. Digging up the roots in their entirety is tough as they tend to snap off, leaving deep roots, and the vinegar effectively gets to the bottom of the problem.

While 30 percent vinegar is my go-to solution for weeds that have already sprouted, I prefer to prevent them in the first place. That's right, the best line of defense is always a good offense! I do my best to make it difficult for them to grow at all, and a thick bed of mulch works very well for that purpose. Plants need two things to grow: water and sunlight. A thick layer of mulch starves the seeds from the sunlight they need to germinate. It's simple and effective, and the one variant that impacts its effectiveness is the thickness of the mulch layer—the thicker, the better. I've found that two to three inches of mulch deprives seeds and roots from the sun and warmth they need to germinate and grow. And it sure saves the time and headache of trying to get rid of the weeds after they show up, which is when they are most difficult to manage.

Granted, the occasional weed will get through your mulch and there might be some seeds that land on top layer of much and manage to grow, but they are manageable, and the mulch keeps them to a minimum.

That said, what type of mulch do I recommend? Yes, there is more than one type of mulch ... and all mulch is not created equally. I like to use a shredded version called gorilla hair mulch, which won't blow in the wind like mulch chips will, and I always prefer to get mulch that is not colored, as the chemicals used to color the mulch will leach off into the soil. I also steer clear of rubber mulches as they are laden with chemicals. The bonus of using a natural product like wood mulch is that it not only prevents weeds, but it also benefits the soil and plants because it helps the soil maintain moisture and enriches the soil as it decomposes.

Rocks can be effective in preventing weeds, but there are some challenges here. Rock is expensive, so landscapers generally put a thin layer of larger rocks to just cover the ground. This provides a nice aesthetic and ample access for weed seeds to moisture, warmth, and light, allowing them to easily germinate. The most common way this is addressed is to add a layer of landscape fabric or plastic underneath. In very short order, these will tear, and the weeds make their way through, anyway, defeating the purpose. Within six months, you are on your hands and knees pulling weeds—ask me how I know! Have we won this battle with nature? Not even close, she has us pinned and the ref is counting.

Big rocks leave big gaps, so a deep layer of small rocks with few air gaps would yield better results. Skip the barrier underneath, those make it easier for the roots to stay alive underneath and more difficult to pull any weeds that do come through. Additionally, the barriers deny oxygen to the soil, impeding the microscopic life that lives in the soil from thriving, and ultimately less healthy soil.

Rocks are a naturally occurring thing, so how can they be bad? They aren't. Big sheets of plastic across soil I might call bad, but a monoculture of rocks in an area can be challenging from a weed control standpoint. Rocks are champs at holding onto heat, so when deciding where you want to place rocks, consider what else is around. Rocks placed next to the foundation of a home are great for drainage and aesthetics, not so good for your cooling bill in summer.

"Hey, Dee!"

Commonly-asked Questions

1. Hey, Dee: I already have a rock area, and I can't afford to change it right now. How do I get rid of the weed barrier underneath?

   Grab your shovel! When we bought our house in Colorado, it had rock in several areas and a weed barrier underneath, which wasn't working. Use a shovel to pull the rocks back and start tearing it out. If you are able, consider mulch or plantings for the exposed area, and use the removed rock to thicken the remaining rocks to manage the weeds. You don't have to do it all at once, a little at a time works just fine.

2. Hey, Dee: I don't have a lot of time for yard maintenance, and it sounds like some of these strategies take a long time to implement. What can I do?

   I know this a lot to take in. Pick one or two things to try, maybe try them in just the front yard and add the back yard later. You can do this!

3. Hey, Dee: I have been effectively using some environmentally sound methods you don't mention here. Should I switch?

   Only if the methods I mention are safer and more effective! Please write me at heydee@selfpacedsustainability.com *and tell me what you are doing!*

Avoid, Reuse, Repurpose, Compost, Recycle, Landfill

7 PETS WITH PURPOSE

Growing up in the country, our pets always had a purpose. We had dogs, cats, and goats. Our animals always lived outside, so I grew up with ideas that are not so common these days—animals having a job and living outside. They do, after all, have teeth, claws, and horns and are always outdoor ready because they always have their coats on. (I credit my sister-in-law, Buck, with that little joke. I think it's hilarious!) One of the reasons we have some of the pest control issues we have is that the natural pest control that other critters provide is not available to us when we keep animals indoors. Cats providing mouse and gopher control and dogs harassing everything from squirrels to snakes and coyotes from your property becomes impossible when they are fat and happy napping on the couch. As a kid, we never had problems with most pests because we always had two large dogs (we favored German Shepards) and a multitude of cats living outside to keep everything under control. The goats had the job of keeping the weeds down.

Cats, Cats, and More Cats!

I have always loved cats. I come from a long line of cat lovers and assume that one day I will be a crazy old cat lady, if only my allergies would allow it. At one point, my desire to have pets (particularly cats) came to a head. Our property in Southern California was rural, and we needed cats for pest control purposes, so I decided to adopt some feral cats. I thought I knew what a feral cat was, but it turns out once again that I was wrong.

Growing up, we always had some number of cats, and they lived outdoors, like all our animals. Those cats were barn cats, not house cats; my dad was firmly against letting any of the animals inside unless we were rescuing another litter of kittens and had to bottle feed them for a while. Some of our cats were tame, more like traditional pets, while there were others that were wild and avoided human interaction altogether. That was okay because they required very little human care other than putting food out once in a while (they ate mostly on their own) and making sure they had water. The tradeoff was that our property was pest free—there were no mice, rats, gophers, etc.

When it was time to adopt some ferals, I contacted several organizations that provide feral cats and found out their requirements: a place to confine the animals for four to six weeks with food, water, and litter boxes before turning them loose on your property. The purpose is to acclimate them to the property so they will be less likely to run away when they're set free. I had a chicken coop that had never been used, so we were in business. Of course, I dubbed the chicken coop "The Cat House." I think I was the only one who thought that was funny, but I nevertheless cracked up every time I said it.

Within a few days, a young gal who volunteered for the organization brought four very unhappy cats to our house. I thought they were unhappy because they didn't like the car ride, but one of these cats was a hissing, snarling Tasmanian devil that took a large chunk out of this young lady's hand. They were no barn cats; they were wild beasts!

I felt so sorry for these cats (we named them all after Star Wars characters – Princess Leah, Vader, Obi Wan, and Kylo). We didn't actually know the gender of any of them—it was way too risky to try and find out! Over the next few weeks, we got somewhat used to each other and the routine of feeding and box cleaning and talking to them in a soothing voice several times a day. I felt so sorry for them for being trapped in that small coop, I let them out at four weeks. We kept the coop door open to give them a safe place to retreat and kept food and water out for them. We never saw two of them again. I like to think they just ran off into the wild and lived happily ever after. The other two came home frequently at first, then less often. We discovered that Princess Leah had adopted some neighbors down the road and kept their property pest free. I would see her from time to time and talk to her—although she was our most vicious hisser (and I think the one who took the chunk out of that poor girl's hand), she ended up being rather tame and for quite a few years, she came by from time to time asking for water and a snack. We wouldn't see her for months, and then she would just show up on the porch one day and quietly wait to be noticed. Obi Wan would come by to say hello from time to time for a couple of years, then nothing.

In the end, I think those cats had a better life in our rural area than they would have had contained at a cage at the cat rescue, and certainly better than being euthanized, which is likely where they were headed. It was a valuable learning experience for me—the difference between an indifferent barn cat and a feral is substantial and may require stitches.

When I've had outdoor cats, whether they are feral or barn cats, I haven't had any issues with mice or rats. If there are any, the cats take care of them. But for the most part, I believe that the mere presence of a cat is enough to deter mice from our property, and they voluntarily locate where there is less threat.

Still, an occasional mouse or rat will get by them and scurry into our garage or motorhome. When that happens, I use snap traps because they're fast and don't result in suffering for the animal. (I had a horrific experience with a glue trap and a mouse that was partially stuck to it—I won't say more, except that I won't use those ever again.) I prefer natural deterrents and steer clear of baits and poisons because they pose a risk to pets, as well as other animals or birds of prey who might feed off a dead rodent, causing them to ingest the poison and pass it further on into the food chain.

We currently don't have any cats, mostly because we travel a lot, and as you might guess, we recently noticed an increase of mice in, of all places, our compost bin. Admittedly, I had neglected the bin, and it hadn't occurred to me that mice would be sneaky and find a way to enter into it from the bottom. In all my years of composting I never had mice in my bin, but these determined ones dug not one but two holes under the bin to gain entry. By the time I noticed them, it was too late—word had spread and other mice had joined them. I had to do something and fast before a whole colony erupted in there. First, I tried to determine how many I was dealing with by aerating the bin and adding water. They didn't like that. There were about six of them, a couple of them darted out when the flood started, and I had to get the rest. My husband and I put our heads together and decided a two-pronged approach was necessary. First, a bucket of water in which to drown any we caught. Harsh, I know. I wish I had a better idea, but one just was not forthcoming. We disturbed them and scooped them into the bucket when caught. We then filled in their little tunnels best we could and set snap traps at the entrances. It took a couple of days, but we got them all and they have not returned. I keep encouraging the neighbor's cat to come over and help keep our rodent population in check, so I never have to do that unpleasant task again.

I don't advocate for the killing of any animals. Whenever possible, I let nature keep their populations in check. There are cats, owls, and snakes that feed off mice, but there are times, like this, when I have to step in. Mice just carry too much bacteria and disease, and when they are overpopulated, there is a greater likelihood that one or more of the little critters will find its way into our house ... and I'm not going to let that happen.

Drastic times call for drastic measures, but in my case, those measures will always be free of chemicals and other toxins, and they'll be as swift and painless as possible.

Prevention is always my preferred pest control, and cats, snakes and owls are the best mouse prevention method around. Of course, not all cats are feral or even barn cats. Pumpkin is the perfect example.

Pumpkin the Cat

One day, my daughter called me, clearly upset. A local woman posted on Facebook that she had a mama cat and a new litter of kittens that she did not want, and she planned to dump them at the doorstep of a local vet. She was asking if anyone in the community knew what vets would take them. Keep in mind that this was at 4:00 p.m. on a Saturday in February. I knew that all the vets and humane society were closed for the weekend; it was forecasted to be in the 30's overnight with the possibility of snow. Wherever she ends up dumping these cats, it could well be a death sentence for the kittens and possibly the mother. We couldn't let that happen.

I found the posting on FB and asked the woman to contact me. I met her in the grocery store parking lot and took the cats. I was so angry that someone would consider dumping a mother with a brand-new litter of kittens that I could barely look at the woman. Maybe it's the mom in me that had me so upset, but I felt so bad for that poor mama cat. Scared and alone, she had just given birth and had no home, food, or safety. She gave them to me in a box with a towel covering the top. I pulled it back to reveal a beautiful young Flame Tip Siamese cat—thin as a rail—and her six tiny white fluff balls. I had never had a Siamese cat before—truth be told, I had never wanted one. Siamese cats are probably the neediest of all cat breeds. They want to be with you constantly, are very vocal, and are certainly NOT outdoor cats. CRAP.

We made our guest room the cat room, and the whole family spent many hours those first few days talking to the mama reassuringly, petting her, and making sure she felt safe and secure. I think it was the orange tip of her tail that made me name her Pumpkin. She was very young, maybe 18 months old, but she was an attentive and caring mother. As the weeks passed, the babies' Siamese colors started coming in on all but two of them, who were pure white. And Pumpkin was happy. Her appetite was fierce, but she stayed rail thin. Soon the babies were eating wet food, then dry. They were all little eating machines and, of course, they loved attention. Is there anything cuter than a litter of kittens?

Originally, I had Pumpkin's food, water, and litter box in an area away from her kittens, figuring she could use a few minutes of peace. It didn't take me long to realize that the only way for the kittens to learn to use a litter box properly was to see their mom doing it. Once we moved her litter box in with theirs, we had a whole litter of potty-trained kittens. Easy peasy.

And Pumpkin? She became a member of our family and our only indoor cat, ever. We had other cats that were indoor / outdoor and "earned their keep" hunting regularly. Eventually, Pumpkin expressed a desire to follow us when we sat outside, and unlike other cats, she never wandered away or disappeared. She always came back indoors, living the life of a happy rescued cat. We adopted out all the babies to good homes, and Pumpkin got fixed so she would not have litter after litter. Turns out she was a pretty good mouser once she learned the way of the outdoors, and her coat even turned darker the more time she spent outside. How's that for a natural adaptation! Not coincidentally, we never had an issue with mice when Pumpkin was around; she found her way to being a pet with a purpose.

Dogs

Many people these days select dogs for the purpose of having them live inside the home versus outside. Dogs typically have the job of providing security for the family and property and when outside have the much-added benefit of driving off unwanted pests. The smell of a larger animal in the vicinity of your home will ward off pests like rodents, snakes, and coyotes, especially if there are neighboring properties that do not have outdoor dogs. In order for this to work, the dog must be outside a majority of the time. Can dogs and cats live outside in harmony? Absolutely! Our dogs also provided security for the cats, keeping the coyotes and large birds of prey at bay, extending the life expectancy of our country cats substantially. Our dogs have also been my running partners, horseback riding partners, and when I was growing up, they walked me to the bus stop every morning and patiently waited for the bus to take me away, then returned home to resume their security duties.

Chickens

Chickens are wonderful yard birds and do a great job keeping control of bugs of all kinds with their constant scratching and pecking for food. I didn't learn much about chickens until later in life, since no one in our family kept chickens (come to think of it, none of my friends' families did, either). I was in my 40's when I learned that you don't need a rooster for your chickens to lay eggs. Somewhere along the way, I had heard that old wives' tale and just assumed it was true. It's one of the things that prevented me from keeping chickens, and it was wrong! By the time I figured out my mistake, most of the kids had flown the coop and the demand for eggs in our house was low. Chickens are flock animals so you need to account for keeping three to four minimum, many would say at least six. Depending on the breed of chicken, you can expect them to lay one egg every day or every other day, with production slowing in colder months. That is a lot of eggs! I still think about it often and love the idea of keeping chickens, but now that we are empty nesters, we are resisting being tied down by any animals working or otherwise. So, like many other people, we have bug problems! Chickens come in handy for keeping garden pests under control, like grasshoppers, squash beetles, and lawn grubs. Can a chicken be a pet? I say yes, and I think anyone who has kept chickens would say they are funny little characters with their own personalities. My friend has kept chickens, ducks, and turkeys, even hatched them from eggs. Her kids name each one and form a bond with their working flocks that provide meat and eggs for the family.

Goats

Did I say goats? Yes, we had two goats on our little farm when I was a kid. Goats are adorable and a lot of fun, but they can also get into a lot of trouble! My parents bought an adult female and had her bred so we would have a baby. Oh, man, was that kid cute (pun intended)! I was a kid myself, so she was my oft companion. When they are little, they will stay close to mom, so baby would run loose and mom would be "staked out." You must find a way to contain a goat, as they are single-minded eating machines. My parents' property was a little over two acres, much of it wild, so there was a lot for the goats to eat; but we also had fruit trees, planted areas, and a vegetable garden we didn't want them to eat. My dad had a large metal stake, maybe 1-1/2" thick steel, he would use to control mama's reach. Make no mistake, a goat is STRONG and determined when there is something they want. We wanted the baby to keep her horns for self-defense from coyotes as she grew, but the grass is always greener on the other side of the fence as they say. The fence between my parents' house and the neighbor on one side was made of hog wire, maybe 4"x 4" or 6"x 6" – just big enough for the baby to get her head through and get her horns stuck when she tried to come back through. When I got off the school bus that day (maybe 1/8 mile away from our long driveway), I could hear both mama and baby bleating in distress. I ran home and cut the fence to free the panicked kid. I never found out how long she was stuck, but none of the neighbors came to the rescue so probably not long. We were lucky that the distress call did not attract the attention of the local coyote population, but it was time to come up with another arrangement. Plan B was to stake baby out near mama but not so close they could get tangled. Between the dogs standing guard, the cats on patrol, and goats on landscaping duty, things were calm, pest and weed free most of the time.

All our pets with purpose have crossed the rainbow bridge, and we have not replaced them. We are empty nesters in the truest sense! It is a stage of life where we are relishing our freedom, and I am sure that eventually we will return to having more furry friends. For now, we are considering adding owl boxes on our rural property to help encourage the circle of life, and we might have to set more snap traps than we want to.

Avoid, Reuse, Repurpose, Compost, Recycle, Landfill

8 NOW YOU'RE COOKING!

Have you heard of a solar oven or maybe even used one? I have, and I'm here to tell you that these things are AWESOME. What is a solar oven? Well, it's just like it sounds: Solar = sun, and oven = a thing to cook food in. It's an oven that uses the power of the sun to cook your food, no solar panels are required! Think outdoor crockpot, without the need for fuel or electricity, or hooking it up to anything. Sounds too good to be true, doesn't it?

I am by nature a skeptic, especially when something sounds too good to be true, and I am never the first to adopt something new—I let it marinate for a while, do my research, and, of course, experiment. I had heard of solar ovens and was intrigued, but very skeptical. There wasn't a lot of information available online at the time, and I had so many questions. Still, I couldn't deny that I was impressed with the benefits of cooking with solar ovens.

People have enjoyed outdoor cooking on grills and wood fires since time began. However, these options, while producing some very tasty results, have environmental impacts and require fuel inputs like propane, gas, wood, or charcoal. Solar ovens, on the other hand, do not require any kind of outside fuel, and they emit no greenhouse gases, because they require only sunlight to work, so there is no negative environmental impact. Still sounds too good to be true, doesn't it? Time to do some research.

Here are some of the questions I had when I started this journey, and I bet you have some of the same questions:

1. How much does a solar oven cost?
2. What kinds of solar ovens are there, and what are the differences?
3. How sunny does it need to be for this thing to work?
4. Do I have to keep turning it, so it always has full sun in order for it to work? Because, if so, who's got time for that?
5. Will animals be attracted by the smell of the food as it cooks, and will the hungry critters come to my deck and knock it over, carrying my dinner away while I'm at work?
6. Will it cook meat fully? I don't want salmonella or botulism or whatever.
7. What if it's not hot enough to cook it to the point where it's safe to eat?
8. How long does it take to cook something all the way?
9. Will it overcook my food if I'm not there to watch it?

When solar ovens first became available for purchase, there weren't many places to find the answers to all my questions. It wasn't until I met a vendor who was demonstrating and promoting solar ovens that I got the answers I needed and an education about solar ovens, how they work, and the different ways I could use them (with recipes to boot!). In this chapter, I share that information and my experience as the owner of three solar ovens.

A Word on Green Washing

There is a lot of green washing out there when it comes to things that are marketed as environmentally friendly. Green washing is when a company markets something as "green" or "environmentally friendly" with little to no proof or evidence that it is true. Sometimes, the opposite is true. Those of us that spend a lot of time in the sustainability world always have our radar on high alert for green washing. When I started this investigation, I was highly skeptical but ended up pleasantly surprised.

1. **How much does a solar oven cost?**

    While most solar ovens are not outrageously expensive (although I have seen a glass tube version that not only cooked unreasonably small portions of food, but it was also outrageously expensive), they start at about $50 and go up to about $600, depending on type / size model. I can vouch for the two different types that I have used the most: a solar reflector model and a hot box model. I have used them both extensively and love them!

    Prices can and likely will fluctuate as the technology, size, and competition change over time. However, one thing will not change, and that is the fact that when using a solar oven, you will not pay anything for fuel or any type of connection as it needs none at all!

2. **What kinds of ovens are there, and what are the differences?**

   Reflector Type Ovens:

   The reflector type is very portable as it can fold flat for storage/transit and is a simple foam board style with a reflective foil-like interior. This is a great option for camping or putting in a work truck to heat up your lunch. It is adjustable for different azimuths of the sun to optimize solar reflection and is very quick and easy to set up. When I bought this one, it was in the $100 range and was made by a local solar oven scientist / inventor in San Diego, CA. I was able to take a solar cooking class from him, and he answered all those burning questions I had and gave me the confidence to buy my first solar oven and give it a try.

   Many solar ovens require the use of black Dutch oven type dishes for cooking. They do not have to be heavy-duty cast iron. In fact, you are better off with a very light-duty version.

   The important features are:

   a. black (you want it to be dark so it will attract and hold the heat better)

   b. have a lid

   It's even better if there is a lip around the edge so you can clip the lid to the pot while cooking. The contents will get so hot while cooking, it will form steam and the lid will bounce around letting the heat out, just like in a traditional oven! I use metal office style bunder clips to keep the lids on. I got both the oven and the cooking dishes on Amazon. This version of oven also requires the use of an oven bag to put the Dutch oven in while cooking. It helps trap the heat/steam that is generated and keep the cooking temperature from dropping. Yes, I know the bag is plastic. I know, I know—the best you can do here is wash it and reuse it. Will some other more sustainable option work? I would love to hear your ideas!

I have cooked excellent meat and vegetable / side dishes in this oven. I tend to cook larger volumes of food (we like leftovers for lunches), so if there were a drawback to this oven, it is that I can only fit one large dish in at a time. A note of caution: this oven is very lightweight, so it only took me a minute to figure out I needed to add a few rocks into the oven bottom to hold it down in the afternoon winds, so make sure you weigh it down, or your dinner might go flying across the yard.

I call my solar ovens my outdoor crockpots, because they cook the same way, only without the cord. Just like a crock pot, you put the solar oven out in the morning, and you come home to a warm, delicious, cooked dinner. I have found that the more liquid you have, the longer it takes to cook. For meat lovers, you can put in a few chicken breasts or a roast with spices and no liquid, and when you get home, you have very tasty meat for dinner. There is something about long, slow cooking in the solar oven that adds an incredible baked flavor – delicious! This type of oven is best for either cooking one thing at a time or putting several items into the same dish to cook together like a casserole.

Hot Box Type Ovens

About a year after getting my reflector oven, I decided I wanted another oven, but I wanted to try a different type. I chose the hotbox type because it was not too expensive but would provide enough room for me to cook two large Dutch ovens, instead of one. I have often cooked larger meals using both ovens at the same time.

This hot box style solar oven is sometimes referred to as a solar box cooker. It is different from a reflector oven in that it has its own clear lid that covers the top, so no oven bags are needed. BONUS: I found a way to avoid plastic bags with this oven! This oven is heavy enough on its own that no rocks are needed, but not too heavy for me to carry by myself.

I have made chicken, roast beef, rice, vegetables, spaghetti sauce – you can cook just about anything in a solar oven that you can cook on a stove or in an oven. No energy from your home is required, and when it's hot outside, there's no need to heat your house up to make a meal. While some people use their solar oven occasionally, such as when camping, during a power outage, etc., I have read about people who almost exclusively use their solar ovens, which is certainly an option. I've been very happy with the convenience and results. Mine is a Solavore price point ~ $200. I am unclear about the status of this brand; it may be discontinued. The closest item I can find readily available is the All-American Sun Oven. It has great reviews but comes with a hefty price tag ~ $550.

There are other types of solar ovens available, some look like a satellite dish, and you put your cooking pot in the middle; it concentrates the sun onto your cooking area. These appear to be rather heavy (over 30 pounds), so they aren't very portable but fine for cooking at home. Price point: $75-100 on Amazon.

There is also the tube type (remember back in the day of the drive-through bank teller and you put your transaction into the tube and a vacuum system sucked it over to the teller?). These ovens work by putting your food in the teller tube, but instead of making a bank deposit, it sits in the sun and cooks, then you pull it back out. These are reputed to work well but inspect the dimensions closely. Many of these hold a very small amount of food, fine for one person. More recent additions to the marketplace claim to hold enough for two to three people. These look to be a good option for baking as the cooking temperatures are high and they retain heat well. Weight ~ 13.5 pounds, price point is $200 on Amazon. I just bought one and am looking forward to trying it. Stay tuned for some updates on this one!

So, I bet some of you still have some of the same questions I once had, yes? I will answer them for you here.

> **How sunny does it need to be for this thing to work?** *ANS: You need a minimum of 20 minutes of sun per hour, so it can be used on partially sunny days. Outside temperature does not matter, I am told. I have not tried to cook in the arctic sun.*
>
> **Do I have to keep turning it so it's always exposed to full sun? Because if so, who's got time for that?** *ANS: Nope. Place it properly in the morning (full sun, facing toward the sun at the time you want cooking to start) and you are done. Make sure you weigh down the lighter weight solar ovens.*

Will animals be attracted by the smell of the cooking food and knock it over, carrying my dinner away while I'm at work? *ANS: I can't say they won't smell it, but it's far too hot for them to bother with it. I have lots of wildlife regularly trekking through my property and have never had a problem. I'm not dealing with bears, though – we have bobcats, racoon, fox, coyote, and dogs. I've heard of lots of people using solar ovens when camping, but I can't vouch for any experience they might or might not have had with bears.*

Will it cook meat enough to be fully cooked and safe? I don't want salmonella or botulism or whatever. What if it's not hot enough to cook it all the way? *ANS: Cooking time varies, depending on what you are cooking and the type of solar oven you're using. Data shows that reflector-type solar ovens can cook up to 338 degrees, and the hotbox models cook foods at temperatures up to 392 degrees. Regardless of which type you use, you can cook a turkey in a single day with one of these. If you are short on time, check your solar cookbook for minimum cooking time and plan accordingly. I cooked large roasts with no problem in six hours. Cooking times are somewhere between that of an oven and a crock pot. If you have a situation where you didn't end up with enough sunlight to fully cook something, you can pop it into a traditional oven and finish it.*

How long does it take to cook something all the way? *ANS: see #4 above*

Will it overcook my food if I'm not there to watch it? *ANS: Nope. Because it works somewhat like an outdoor crockpot and the sun's path changes throughout the day, the intense high heat time is a few hours, then it begins to cool as the day goes on. It will stay warm for a time after the sun goes down but don't leave your food out there too long or you may lose your dinner to some local wildlife.*

Notes on Solar Cooking

Box cookers are the most widespread type of solar oven used around the world. They are used daily in refugee camps and other places where energy and other cooking sources aren't available.

I recommend choosing a solar oven that meets your storage and portability needs. If you're traveling, camping, or hiking, select a model that folds compactly—much like a large notebook that you can carry in a backpack.

You can cook nearly anything in a solar oven. You can fry food in some of the newer models. About the only thing I've tried that didn't really work out well was hard-boiled eggs. Technically, you don't need water to hard boil eggs in a solar oven. Just put the eggs in the Dutch oven and let her rip. They cooked completely, no issues there. When peeled, however, they had a brown tint, instead of white – the book told me this would happen, so I wasn't too concerned. I didn't like the way they tasted, though – it was a different taste than eggs boiled in water. To each his own, but I didn't care for it.

You can bake in solar ovens (hot box type), though it requires a little more heat. Manufacturers claim that they can bake cakes and breads with no problem. My oven came with some reflectors that you can mount for this purpose, but I have not tried it yet. I'm not much of a baker because then I want to eat whatever I've baked, and I don't need that kind of help!

Worried about having enough sun? Remember you only need 20 minutes per hour, the rest of the time, it can be cloudy or partially obscured. Even in cooler months these will work if you have some sun. It's not just for the people in Florida and California! I would love to hear from people in colder climates about your solar cooking experiences!

Did you know that you can make your own solar oven? You can! There are kits available that come with everything you need, or you can "Google it" and find a list of materials and instructions to make one totally from scratch—like cooking from scratch! Get the kids involved and make it a science / STEM project and a lesson in sustainability!

I would call my investigation and experimentation with solar cooking a rousing success. The money spent on the ovens and the Dutch ovens to do the cooking was well worth it and can be used over and over for years to come. They may sound too good to be true, but there is no greenwashing here.

Beginner – buy a less expensive solar oven and give it a try! The first one I ever bought is currently listed on Amazon for $106.99, "All Season Solar Cooker Camper." I see options for under $50, but do your homework and read reviews. It is important to select one within your budget that also suits your needs and won't be a waste of money.

Intermediate – dive into that second solar oven! Try a different kind than you already have. Bake your favorite dessert in your solar oven!

Advanced – go all in and make sure you have portable options for camping, traveling, or on the go. Try cooking for a party completely in your solar ovens.

"Hey, Dee!"

Commonly-asked Questions

1. Hey, Dee: Do you teach solar cooking classes?

   I have been recently asked to add this to my repertoire. I have not designed the class yet but stay tuned!

2. Hey, Dee: Can you use a solar oven to warm up food vs. cooking it?

   You bet you can, it just takes less time. Make sure you are using heat safe containers; glass would be best. Remember heated plastic off gasses contaminants into your food, and the temperature in the oven might get too hot for plastic.

3. Hey, Dee – can you boil water in a solar oven?

   You sure can. Even if you didn't integrate your solar oven into your regular routine, having one available for power outages, fires and other emergencies would be a big benefit. You might be one of the few that is prepared in an emergency!

Avoid, Reuse, Repurpose, Compost, Recycle, Landfill

9 THE LAZY COMPOSTER

I have had many friends and students ask if I was going to include an instructional chapter on composting in this book, and it seems like I would be remiss if I did not, since it is such a big part of my sustainability journey. The joy I get from creating compost is a strange feeling that is hard to describe. I experience unabated JOY at adding things into my compost bins, instead of a trash can. I rejoice at the tiny amounts of trash that leave my house, and I know I am making a big difference every time I choose the compost bin, instead of the trash can.

As much happiness as composting brings me, alas, I am a very busy person and don't spend as much time as I would like playing in my compost piles, experimenting with new ideas and new methods. I call myself the lazy composter because it's true! The myth that it takes a lot of time and effort to compost is just not true, and I am living proof. My travel schedule keeps me away from home much of the time, and the many projects and activities scheduled on a regular basis keep me very busy when I am at home. On the occasions that I do get to spend a lot of time with my compost bins or in my garden,

I fantasize about a time when I can spend all day puttering outside doing nothing else but tending my plants and my bins. Someday (cue the dreamy music…)!

The method you will learn here is traditional backyard composting. If you do not have the room required to use this method and want to move on to indoor composting methods, please go to chapter ten: Happy Worms Make More Worms.

I love to teach composting as a live demonstration with my bins and worms and all my materials so I can show people exactly what they can do in their own yard, but I also teach in a classroom environment, so I bring props and use a lot of photos. The looks I get from people as I am hauling my compost crank, various containers, and other items into the local library is fun for me; I like to imagine what they are thinking! To find out when and where I am teaching live, follow our Facebook or LinkedIn group @selfpacedusstainability. If you are unable to take a class from me in person, you can take an on-demand course with video instruction, demonstrations, and downloads that would be a most helpful supplement to this chapter. You can register for the course at https://www.yspe.co/offers/77qqAN3p/checkout and retake it as many times as you like once registered.

Common Questions

- Will it smell?
- Will it attract rodents?
- How long does it take to make finished compost?
- How often do I have to tend my bin?
- How will I know when my compost is ready?
- Can I put worms in my outdoor bin?
- What kind of things should I avoid putting in my bin?

- Can I put packaging paper in my bin?
- Where should I locate my bin?
- How do I gather and manage browns/ carbons?
- How do I gather and manage greens/nitrogens?

All these burning questions and quite a few more will be answered in this chapter. Let's get started!

What is Composting?

Composting is the natural process of decomposition of organic material. When we compost, we are controlling and accelerating this natural process to create nutrient rich soil. Composting is an aerobic process, meaning with air. There are four required inputs to a compost bin to make composting work:

1. Carbons or browns
2. Nitrogens or greens
3. Moisture
4. Oxygen

The terms carbons and browns are used interchangeably, as well as nitrogens and greens, in the world of composting.

What are Browns/Carbons?

- Anything that was once a living plant but is now dead on its way to dead is a brown. This includes dead leaves, sticks, wood, paper, cereal boxes, magazines, catalogs, junk mail, packaging, cardboard, newspaper or any paper products, and dead plants. Nature helps us out for the most part here by naturally turning dead plants brown.
- Coconut shells, pinecones, cotton clothes, dryer lint, vacuum cleaner contents, human hair, animal hair, bird feathers.

- Used tissues and paper towels.

It all composts over time! Some of the more robust items like pinecones and coconut shells may take longer; we will touch on that later.

What have I tried and failed? Palm fronds and pine needles. Palm fronds are very thick, not to mention they have edges that are sharp as a razor, and I don't recommend putting those in your bin. Pine needles have a waxy coating on them that make them very slow to decompose and will stab you when you put your hands in the bin. They will compost eventually, but it's measured in years, and meanwhile good luck harvesting your finished compost with these mixed in. It is also important to note that pine needles inhibit the growth of many other plant species, so you won't want these in your garden, anyway.

What are Greens/Nitrogens?

- Plants or plant parts that are living, or mostly living, like fruit and vegetable kitchen scraps, lawn clippings, live or semi-live leaves (items transition from greens to browns as they die), plant trimmings, eggshells, seeds, nuts, coffee grounds, vegetarian dishes.
- Manure from vegetarian animals, such as cows, horses, rabbits, goats, etc.
- Birds are technically omnivores, but their manure is acceptable for a compost pile. Ducks, chickens, and pet birds' manure are a great source of nitrogen.
- Moldy leftovers from the fridge, freezer burned stuff from the back of the freezer, no problem if they don't contain meat or dairy.

- Fun fact – human urine is sterile if you are healthy and free of medications. It is also an excellent source of nitrogen! Some people choose to use urine as a source. You decide!

Inputs to Avoid

- Meat and dairy - the decomposition process for these items is different and will make your bins stinky and slimy. You can use a process called Bokashi for these products, which I touch upon in chapter 11. Check my YouTube channel for Bokashi updates: www.youtube.com/@yellowstoneprofessionaled

- Carnivore waste (dog, cat) – carnivore waste has pathogens that are hazardous to humans and contaminate your edible plants.

- Weeds – unless you are using a method of composting called hot pile (which is not a method I typically teach as it is high maintenance in comparison), the weed seeds will not be killed off and will proliferate in your compost.

- Plastics

- Pine needles

- Palm leaves

- Oils

- If you have worms in your compost bin, avoid all oils and citrus. Worms breathe through their skin and if coated by oil, they will suffocate. Citrus is a great natural cleaner and disinfectant; the same properties also burn the skin of the worms. My compost bins are large and have earthen contact so my worms can leave if they don't like something that is present. Because of this, I do put small amounts of citrus in my bins. We will talk more about bins later in this chapter.

Storage and Preparation of Browns

I have used many different containers for this over time, and I have settled on a couple of very useful ones to share with you. You will need at least one, possibly two containers, depending on the workflow you prefer and how attentive you want to be to this process. Remember, browns are all going to be clean and dry, so storage is a little simpler than with greens. It is important to note the primary container size must be watertight with handles, and you must be able to lift it full of water, so don't go too big for container one.

- Storage container one: I have a 31-gallon Rubbermaid storage tote for my pantry just off the kitchen where I gather browns to be composted. This is paper, cardboard, boxes, junk mail, catalogs, magazines, etc. As the week goes on, I tear the pieces of packaging or paper into smaller pieces. (This is actually pretty good stress relief after a rough day!) The smaller they are, the faster they will decompose, but there is a word of caution here. In the beginning, I was convinced I needed to shred everything. You certainly can if you want to, but I found it just took more time and energy each week and didn't accomplish much. In fact, I ended up with huge clumps and balls of shredded paper in my compost, so it wasn't worth it. Remember that this primary container should be selected for a size you can lift when it is full of water. If that needs to be a bucket size, that is fine. Locate this container so it is convenient for you to use.

My 31-gallon storage tote:

- Storage container two: At certain times of year, we either have an abundance of browns (holidays or in the winter when we may be adding less because of the freezing temperatures) that need storing. You can either use a large trash bag or a supplemental storage container. Composting your personal papers is an excellent way to guard against identity theft. No shredding is required, and it is doubtful that an identity thief will go rifling through your compost to steal your information when there are much easier targets!

Storage and Preparation of Greens

Greens present some challenges that browns do not, in that they are wet, begin decomposing rapidly, and can get quite stinky fast. There are three ways we can deal with this.

1. Store in an airtight container, add to your compost when ready
2. Put in the freezer and add to your compost when ready
3. Put directly in your compost

Since I am the lazy composter, which method do you think I use?

Certainly not #3! I store it in an airtight container right in my kitchen. Though the freezing method is quite effective and creative, I never seem to have extra freezer space for this – congratulations if you do!

I have tried several different countertop containers, including those beautiful stainless-steel ones you can buy online. They have a fatal flaw, however, that is the ventilation holes on top. They usually come with a charcoal filter to prevent smells from getting into your house, which mostly works, but fruit flies are not fooled. When I ended up with a kitchen full of fruit flies, that was a deal killer for me. Retailers being retailers, they also want to sell you plastic or compostable bags to line these containers, which is more cost, more waste, and not necessary.

I settled on a repurposed coffee container. Most coffee doesn't come in metal containers anymore; they come in plastic tubs. One day, I looked at the Folgers containers that I had been saving and using for dry food storage and thought, hey – the snap-on lid is made to be airtight and keep the coffee fresh inside; why wouldn't that keep the smell in from decomposing greens, too? This has worked flawlessly and without odors for many years! They are not nearly as attractive as stainless steel, but if that is a primary concern, you can keep it under the sink or in a roll-out drawer close by.

If you find some other great options that are working for you, I would love to hear from you!

Email me at heydee@selfpacedsustainability.com

Compost Bin Selection

The primary features of a good compost bin are:

- Access to air
- Retention of moisture
- Deter animals
- Attract helpers
- Ease of maintenance

There are dozens of compost bins on the market for purchase, and dozens more options for building your own. This is one of the areas where I see people struggle, and I, too, made some early mistakes here.

Before selecting the bin that is right for you, consider your climate.

The mistake I made with my first compost bin was not having enough knowledge to make the right choice. I got online and read some articles about building your own bin (I can do that; I don't need to buy anything, right?). What I didn't realize is that the articles I was reading were for a completely different climate. I was in a dry climate with little to no rain, and the articles were about very wet climates. Additionally, I was in a rural area with lots of critters that wanted to get into the bin and eat all the greens I am adding; and I proceeded to have a year-long argument with a raccoon. I lost. My bin was made of chicken wire sides held up by metal stakes and had no cover. Way too much access to air for that climate, no ability to retain moisture, no ability to deter animals. Epic fail! I didn't know what I didn't know, but that's okay. I was not deterred. After a year of fighting it, I took a composting class and learned what I needed to know.

Homemade Bin Styles:

Wire and Wood - does not deter animals or retain moisture well. Best for an area with lots of rainfall and few pests. A top could be added to improve the design, limit the open space on the sides.

Open wood – does not deter animals or retain moisture well. Best for lots of rainfall and few pests. Additional sides and a top could be added to improve the design.

Wire – if sides are high as in this photo, may deter animals, will not retain moisture well. This photo shown is on top of a pallet so there is no ability to attract helpers. High sides as shown would make maintenance difficult. This style would be best for an area with a lot of rainfall. Design would be improved by lowering sides and placing directly on the ground to attract helpers, and a cover would help retain moisture.

Store-bought Bin Styles:

Tumbler – this is a very commonly seen compost bin sold at most big box stores, online, and in garden centers. This bin causes many a composter to give up due to lack of success. This style bin has no earthen contact so it has no ability to attract helpers, including the beneficial bacteria that is in the existing soil that is required for composting to work. Without the beneficial bacteria, the process is significantly stunted or does not progress at all. Additionally, it is not easy to maintain. As more wet materials get added to the tumbler, it becomes quite heavy. The user then uses a crank to turn the entire tumbler, which can be hard on the back. In every composting class I have ever taught, there is at least one student that is there because they have one of these and can't figure out why they aren't making compost.

Plastic conical – this is probably the second most common commercial bin I come across. I don't consider this one easy to maintain because the top is so narrow. It's difficult to see what is happening inside, and even more difficult when you go to aerate your bin with tools we will discuss shortly.

Recycled plastic Algreen Soil Saver – I am not sure why every backyard composter out there is not using this bin. This is the only bin I have ever found that checks all the boxes. It is about two feet by two feet, the lid that locks in place is the same size as the bin. (I have not come across a racoon yet that can get into this bin!) It retains moisture well and is five sided (no bottom), so we have earthen contact. The prices run between $110- $175 each. They can be a little elusive to find in stores; in the past, I have found them at Amazon, Home Depot, Tractor Supply, Walmart, and various online gardening supply houses. You can buy direct from the manufacturer at algreenproducts.com/collections/composters/products/soilsaver-composter, and they will often have the best deal. They are easy to put together, and I have had mine for many years.

By the way, I think photos like this are absolutely hilarious. I have tried using the "convenient sliding doors" at the bottom of a bin to harvest compost. It does not work. Besides, when you go to harvest, you will be harvesting the whole bin at once—we will talk more about how to know when to harvest your compost a little later in this chapter. I have provided this photo for entertainment purposes only!

Location, Location, Location

Just like in real estate, it's all about location. WHERE you put your bin is just as important as choosing the right bin for you. Your bin should be:

- Convenient to use
- Close to a water source
- Close to kitchen/ house
- Preferred to have soil contact to allow helpers and good bacteria

Despite what you may have heard, whether your bin is in the sun or shade does not matter. The heat that is produced during the composting process is generated from what is inside the bin. Sun, shade, or partial sun/shade will not impact the composting process.

Bin Helpers and Pests

You will have all kinds of critters show up in your compost bin over time; many of them are helpers or neutral, and a few are pests you want to avoid.

- Helpers / neutrals
    - Worms, pill bugs, sow bugs, soldier fly larvae, roaches (eww, I know, but they will occasionally show up and move along quickly), beetles, mites, mold, fungi, flies, frogs, spiders, grubs.
- Pests
    - Centipedes, millipedes, bees, slugs, ants (a few now and then are fine, but you don't want a colony), earwigs, mice, rats, racoons, squirrels, dogs, coyotes.

A note on rodents – rodents typically like dry and undisturbed places to hide. If you are maintaining your bin properly (keeping it aerated and wet), they aren't likely to hang around. In all my years of composting, I have only had this unpleasant surprise once, and it was because I was not tending my bins enough. It's okay to be a lazy composter, but not too lazy!

I love to see what kinds of things are making a home in my compost bins (as long as they don't have beady eyes and long tails – ewwww). It is constantly changing; one week I will have some fungi growing, and next week I might have some frogs. Spiders and pill bugs are frequent visitors, along with gnats and flies, especially in summer. Worms may show up on their own, or you can add red wigglers to your bin to enrich your compost and speed things up. If you are going to add worms, only do this in bins that have earthen contact, so they have an escape route if they need it. Worms are quite sensitive to moisture and temperature and, as mentioned before, to oils and citrus. You can have worms in your outdoor bin even in cold climates! They come and go as they need to and will come back to your bin as a known source of food when the conditions are right.

Tool Selection for Bin Aeration

The availability of air to your compost pile is only partially addressed with the type of bin you choose. Composting requires active aeration from you, the composter, on a regular basis. As with any task, having the proper tools for the job is a key factor to success. When selecting the proper tools, consider:

- Length: how much bending will be required. If you are small like me, perhaps not much but a long tool for me would present a problem.
- Construction: I like my tools to be sturdy. You are going to be using them for a long time, it is worth it to invest in good quality that will last.
- Motion required: for the bin type you have selected.

Shovel / pitchfork - You may already have these in the garage. I have used both and do not prefer them for aeration, but I do use a shovel for harvesting.

Winged pole? - There is a style I find at almost every garden center with a long handle and tiny wings on the bottom that fold and unfold. The intent is that you use the little wings to aerate the contents of your bin. I think it might take you something close to forever to properly aerate an entire compost bin with one of these, especially if it is in early stages of decomposition.

Screw aerator – there are a few styles of these, my favorite is the Lotech compost crank. It is made of stainless steel, so this lazy composter can leave it lying beside the compost bins outside year round, and the motion to use it is easy on the back (wet compost gets heavy!). It is made from recycled materials and is very durable. The price point is about $85-$95, and I have never found it in a brick-and-mortar location, so online we go. Occasionally, I see them on Amazon, but you can always order from the manufacturer at https://www.lotechproducts.com/products/compost-crank-compost-aerator

Starting a Compost Bin

Look at all the hard work you have done so far! You have learned:

- What composting is and what is needed to achieve it
- What appropriate greens and browns are
- How to store your greens and browns
- What to avoid putting into your bins and why
- The pluses and minuses of various compost bin styles
- Proper bin selection for your circumstances
- Proper bin location
- Proper tool selection

Now it's time to start your first compost bin!

1. Bring your container of torn browns outside and set them down on the ground near your compost bin. Drag over a hose and fill the browns container with water, soaking the browns and let it sit for a few minutes. This will help raise the moisture level of your browns and keep your materials moist inside the compost bin.

2. Bring out your containers of greens. You are going to want approximately a 60/40 ratio of browns to greens. It's okay to have more browns—if you have to err, err on the side of more browns.

3. Add a few small sticks to the bottom of your compost bin, right on top of the dirt. This will help keep the next layer from

getting too friendly with the dirt just yet.

4. Add about half of the volume of your soaked browns on top of the sticks.

5. Add all the greens.

6. Add the second half of the soaked browns. Dump any additional water onto the pile.

7. Cover and lock your bin; you have started your first compost bin!!

The initial start of a bin is somewhat different than what you will do when adding later. You will notice we did not aerate on the initial start, that comes later with bin maintenance. Leaving these nice wet layers on top and bottom with the greens sandwiched in between will get things started. The more volume you have in your bin, the easier it will retain moisture. In these early days with a small volume, particularly in a drier climate, you will need to pay a little more attention to your bin.

If you live in an area that is subject to windy conditions, an empty bin or a nearly empty bin can become a flying object. It took me quite a while to become convinced I needed to do something to keep them from flying across the yard on a gusty day—there is nothing quite like seeing a compost bin flying by your window (think Wizard of Oz). I can personally attest that the Soil Savers are sturdy and have survived my learning curve well. With a few screws, they are still serving their purpose years later. Some large rocks on the lid and a few stakes at the bottom corners prevent me from having to visit the Wizard (or my neighbors' yards) to get my bins back.

Compost Bin Maintenance

After the initial start of your bin, you can add greens and browns on your schedule, keeping in mind that you want to maintain a ratio of about 60% carbon to 40% nitrogen, erring on the side of carbon. It is okay to add greens without adding browns if you stay in this balance. Too many greens will produce a smelly, slimy bin. If this happens, add more soaked browns and aerate.

You don't necessarily need to aerate every time you dump some greens in the bin but do aerate anytime you add browns to mix them together. For video demonstrations of bin maintenance, visit my YouTube channel at youtu.be/7orcQBpC-Vk?feature=shared

Make sure you add moisture and aerate thoroughly, getting all the dry edges and corners. The contents of your bin need to stay moist for decomposition to start and continue. This is why a bin with somewhat solid sides can be helpful and is certainly lower maintenance—it helps to keep the moisture in, so you can add it less frequently. Adding water once per week while tending your bin is enough, but when you are just getting started, you may need to add moisture every few days until you build some volume.

Full bin maintenance typically 1-2 times per week:

1. Aerate thoroughly
2. Add moisture (do these alternately as you can see in the demonstration videos in the online class or on our You Tube channel). Some aeration, exposing the dry parts of the bin, add water, more aeration, add more water.
3. Once thoroughly moist and aerated, add nitrogens, aerate them into the bin contents.

4. Add wetted carbons as a nice insulating layer on top to help keep the moisture in.

The whole process takes 10-15 minutes most weeks. As your bin approaches full, steps 1 and 2 may take a little longer. You will notice as the weeks go by that the bin level will drop as decomposition is happening. How long it will take you to completely fill one bin will depend on the amount of waste you are diverting. It typically takes 10-12 months for a bin to become full for me.

Why Three Bins?

When you see a composting set up, you usually see three bins in a row. Why is that? The only way to get finished compost is to stop adding to that bin. At the 10– to 12-month mark when I see that my bin has reduced as much as it's going to and it's full, I stop adding to it and start a new one. After starting your second bin, you still need to add moisture and aerate the first one until you have completed compost. The bin you are adding carbons and nitrogens into is called your active bin. The bin you have stopped adding to but is not yet done is the cooking bin, and the third bin either holds finished compost or has been harvested and is waiting to be the next active bin. When you are starting your composting journey, you need only start with one bin and can add bins as you progress.

Bin placement note – ensure you leave enough space between and around your bins for maintenance. I space my bins about two feet apart and have space on all sides so I can walk all the way around to make aerating easier.

Finished Compost

How long will it take? Depending on the state of your bin and frequency of maintenance, two to four months AFTER you stop adding carbons and nitrogens. You will know it is done when there is no more identifiable waste in the bin; it just looks like dark brown, rich, beautiful dirt! If you have a few items that are more robust, like pinecones or coconut shells, that remain while everything else is done, just move those items to your next active bin. Do not forget to continue to add moisture and aerate as the bin is cooking, or you may not ever get finished compost!

Troubleshooting

- Bad smells
    - Animal products like meat or dairy have been added
    - Not enough carbons
    - Too much moisture
- Unwanted critters
    - Bin too dry
    - Not sealed from animal intrusion
    - Inadequate aeration
- Slow progress
    - Not enough moisture
    - Inadequate aeration
    - Not enough nitrogen
    - Tumbler bin – add a shovel full of native soil to add beneficial bacteria

There are many variables to composting, depending on your climate and the time and energy you want to invest. Composting doesn't have to be a chore; in fact, it can be quite fun! Even lazy composters like me can be successful composters if they follow the basic guidelines outlined in this chapter.

Composting at your pace and your way:

1. **Beginner**: Buy or build one bin and get started using the instructions in this chapter.

2. **Intermediate**: Start experimenting with different materials in your bin, add some worms to help things along and add another dimension of interest to your routine.

3. **Advanced**: Add Bokashi to your food waste diversion game!

"Hey, Dee!"

Commonly-asked Questions

1. Hey, Dee: Do the inks used in magazines and catalogs and other printed media cause a problem?

   Most inks these days are soy based, so they are not nearly as much of a concern as they used to be. Avoid shiny metallic paper and glitter; otherwise, you are good to go!

2. Hey, Dee: When do you add dirt?

   Never! Well, almost never. A traditional bin does not require it, but this is a trick that works with tumblers since they have no access to soil.

3. Hey, Dee: What if I go on vacation or travel and can't tend my bin weekly?

   You are preaching to the choir! I travel extensively for work and often leave my bins for weeks or even months. This slows the process, but it can easily be restarted by resuming bin maintenance.

4. Hey, Dee: Should I wear gloves?

   This is up to you. Despite my self-declared germaphobia, for some reason, this does not seem to apply to my compost bins. I don't wear gloves, but you do what makes you comfortable!

5. Hey, Dee: What if I have a tumbler bin?

   If you want to keep it, add that shovel of dirt and keep at it, but remember you must stop adding to get finished compost. I recommend moving on to a bin style that provides you with soil contact.

6. Hey, Dee: What if plastic gets into my bin? Do I have to throw out the whole thing and start over?

   Nope! No matter how hard I try, it seems that some kind of plastic makes it into my bins. Plastic you never knew was there will show itself as the paper decomposes. Just pull it out and keep going!

7. Hey, Dee: It snows where I live; can I still compost?

   You sure can! In the winter when the bins freeze, I continue to add greens and hold off on the browns until it's warm enough to aerate, which is when I resume normal bin use and maintenance. Pro tip – snow is an excellent source of moisture in the winter and spring!

Avoid, Reuse, Repurpose, Compost, Recycle, Landfill

10 HAPPY WORMS MAKE MORE WORMS

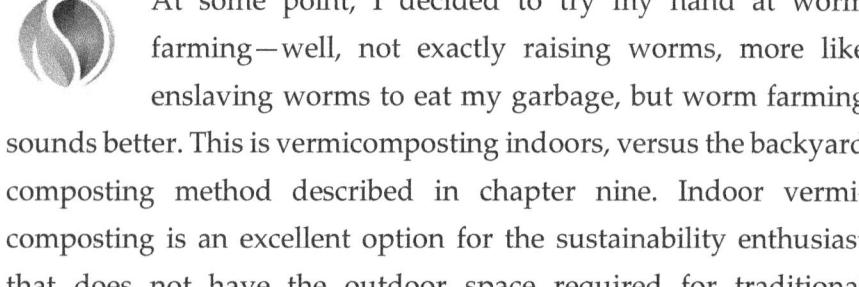At some point, I decided to try my hand at worm farming—well, not exactly raising worms, more like enslaving worms to eat my garbage, but worm farming sounds better. This is vermicomposting indoors, versus the backyard composting method described in chapter nine. Indoor vermicomposting is an excellent option for the sustainability enthusiast that does not have the outdoor space required for traditional backyard composting or just wants to try something new. Vermicomposting produces worm castings (that's a nice way of saying worm poop), one of the most nutrient rich and desirable soil amendments around, commonly referred to as black gold.

Getting Started

You don't need much to get started vermicomposting.
- Container for the worms that keep them in, allows airflow and drainage
- Red wiggler worms

- Material for their initial bedding. Shredded newspaper is an excellent and sustainable choice. Coconut coir works but unless it's native to your area, can be quite expensive and require a lot of shipping to reach you. Dried leaves or aged compost also work.

When I started, I dove in, knowing very little about this beyond what I had heard from others. I knew to buy red wigglers and a bin for them to live in. I knew that if I fed them food scraps, they would eat them, that was pretty much it. I took a quick online visit to Amazon, where I purchased a high-rise condo complex for worms (also called a worm factory) and some red wigglers (Uncle Jim's Worm Farm), and I sat back and waited for delivery.

You do not need to buy a high-rise worm condo like I did, in fact, a couple of Rubbermaid totes with lid work just fine. The container should not let in the light (not clear) because worms like the dark. If you go the tote route, you will need to drill some drainage holes in the bottom of one and set it inside the other, so the worms won't drown from too much moisture. You will also want to drill some small ventilation holes into the sides. Make those higher on the tote to discourage escapees. Keep the lid on the worm house to keep it dark, keep moisture in, and prevent wanderers.

When they arrived, I eagerly made sure my worms felt right at home and distributed them on various levels of their new condo complex, which was ready with moist paper, their preferred bedding. But suddenly the thought of hundreds of wriggling worms in my house seemed like a bad idea. Would they get out and start exploring? Was I going to start finding worms in weird places all over the house? I was certainly getting some strange looks from my husband, who typically lets me experiment without much comment, but he wanted to know what room of the house these worms were going to be staying in. I decided to put them in a shady spot on the front porch. I fretted constantly about them being too hot in the summer (I put a piece of cardboard on the top of the bin with ice cubes to cool them down) or too cold in the winter (I wrapped them in blankets). Much to my husband's dismay, I brought them into the house for periods of time.

My cold feet about having worm roommates was unwarranted. They are quiet, keep to themselves, and never throw loud parties. I had no problems with them when they were in the house, and ultimately, I was making this much harder than it needed to be. I should have just found a quiet corner in the house and let them be. Reflecting on it now, I know just the spot.

Feeding and Care

Worms are sensitive to temperature and need to stay moist, as they breathe through their skin. Some moisture will come from the food scraps you add; the rest can be added using a spray bottle. Bedding should fill about 2/3 of the space and be damp like a wrung-out sponge.

Adding food is as easy as putting kitchen scraps in and closing the lid. If you are using the worm condo, typically you will have a level where you add food, leaving the other levels for nesting and resting. In a tote, add food to one area at a time.

Worms can eat fruit and vegetable scraps, apart from citrus. They also will eat coffee grounds, eggshells, paper, and especially love cardboard to nest in. I swear my worms love summer when they get their favorite treat, watermelon!

Worms need to remain at temperatures between 55-77 degrees F (13-25 degrees C). Putting them in the sun or in cold temperatures can have disastrous results! It is best to keep them inside in a controlled temperature space. Many people use their basement, under a sink, or in a spare bedroom or a closet.

If the bedding gets too moist, add more dry bedding. If the bedding gets too dry, spray it with water. Too wet or too dry is bad for worm health and production.

Overfeeding will cause mold, smells, and fruit flies. Let them consume what you provided before you add more. Feed 1-2 times per week.

Things to Avoid

- Citrus will burn their skin. Unlike an outdoor bin, the worms in these kinds of bins can't leave. Do not add citrus of any kind to a vermicomposting container.
- Oils – since worms breathe through their skin, they can be suffocated by oils.
- Meat and dairy

Harvesting

It is important to harvest worm castings and clean the bins regularly to maintain a healthy environment for your worm helpers. There are several methods of separating your worms from the castings when it comes time to harvest.

- Screening / sifting – dump your container out on a screen or sifter to help separate the worms from the castings.
- Layering – if you have a multiple layer condo style, the food layer will be where most of the worms hang out to make separation easier.
- Tote – put something they really dig (like watermelon) in one corner. Once they have moved to it, relocate the bundle of

worms and watermelon to their new clean container while you pick out the malingerers from the remaining castings.

- More than likely, some combination of these techniques will work for you.

Troubleshooting

Pests – if you are attracting fruit flies, reduce the quantity of scraps you are putting in and bury the scraps in the bedding. Ants? Make sure you have enough moisture. Mites? Add eggshells to balance the pH.

Escapees – this is a sign that something is amiss. Check moisture levels, temperature. Relocate if necessary.

Bad smells – you may be overfeeding. Feed less, chop scraps into smaller pieces. If you have more scraps than your worms can eat, consider adding more worms or adding an outdoor compost bin. You can also bury scraps directly into garden beds, but be aware if you have dogs and racoons around, they may dig it up. Bury at least 12" deep. You can also cut the bottom out of a coffee can and sink it into a garden bed. Leave the lid exposed and add excess food scraps. Refrain from oils, meat, and dairy in all of these scenarios.

Population is not growing – happy worms make more worms, so if your population isn't growing, there could be several factors. Too high or too low levels of: food, pH, moisture, temperature, or an unmaintained bin. Check these one at a time and resolve as needed.

What About Worm Tea?

Worm tea is made by steeping worm castings into water, much like you would a cup of hot tea, then pouring it on your garden as fertilizer, or spraying it onto a plant to provide an immediate boost to a plant in distress. If you have the worm castings, you can just spread them in the garden to have much the same effect, though it may not be as immediate.

In the end, my husband and I went on vacation and left our grown kids to look after my beloved worm colony I had spent a year fretting over. We came home to a worm ghost town. When not cared for, they will vacate the premises and not leave a forwarding address at best—at worst, they will die. I was very sad and took all my vermicomposting materials that were left and put them in my outdoor compost bins. Then something surprising happened – a little while later, I noticed worms in my outdoor compost bins! As the weeks went by, there were more and more. We had hundreds of them, then thousands! Oh my gosh, I had super worm survivors! This experience taught me so much about vermicomposting, and the best part is I still have the descendants of my original worm colony!

Once I discovered that I was making it more difficult than it had to be, it was quite rewarding. Funny, being a worm farmer still makes me think of someone wearing a straw hat and overalls, though I own neither of these. I always wanted to be a farmer, but I always imagined the livestock would be bigger and it would moo or neigh or something. Whether indoors or out, happy worms make more worms!

This chapter does not really lend itself to beginner, intermediate, or advanced steps, but I hope you will give it a try. If it ends up not being for you, take the beddings and whatever worms you have left and bury them in your garden and give them a little water. More than likely, your worms will be gracing your garden with nutrient rich worm poo for years to come.

"Hey, Dee!"

Commonly-asked Questions

1. Hey, Dee: The worm condo comes with a spigot at the bottom to drain off the extra liquid. Is that worm tea?

   That is called leachate. I have seen much marketing that claims this will give you worm tea, but worm tea is made from worm castings steeped in water, not liquid quickly passing through the various stages of the process. There is some value in leachate, but I would not consider it fertilizer.

2. Hey, Dee: Is it true that if you cut a worm in half, you will get two worms?

   You would be surprised how many times I get asked this question by kids and adults alike! No, you will have one dead worm.

3. Hey, Dee: How long do worms live?

   Thirty days to six months, depending on the type of worm.

Avoid, Reuse, Repurpose, Compost, Recycle, Landfill

11 LET'S GET THIS ZERO-WASTE PARTY STARTED!

Like so many people, I enjoy going to parties and events, and I also love to host gatherings and celebrations for my family and friends. I will admit that at times it can be challenging to integrate group celebrations with my passion for sustainable living. One only needs to visit a community event or the beach on a sunny weekend to get a glimpse of how much waste can be generated when groups of people come together. Trash cans are quickly overflowing with plastic cups, plates, water bottles, flatware, napkins, not to mention wrappers and single-use containers. As the waste headed for the landfills piles up, it spills over and litters the ground and is blown everywhere, spreading the mess throughout the area.

As I witness this unnecessary waste on an epic scale, it affects my ability to fully enjoy the event. Each year, there are millions of community events like fundraisers, races, concerts, festivals, and gatherings of friends and families of all sizes. These events are a source of fun and socialization, competition, and good causes, and as humans we enjoy them very much. Many of these events are organized for the purpose of making profit or generating donations; therefore, the underlying motive is to attract large volumes of people that consume, consume, consume. Quite possibly the last thing considered is the amount of waste that will be generated or what will happen to it when the event is over.

I do dream about inspiring organizations and event planners to be more sustainable; but I need to prioritize the things I am working on. I have a running list of careers I would like to have if I had 100 lives to live, and this is on it. For this lifetime, I remain focused on the events I plan and/or host. Whether the event at our house is large or small, zero waste is always a priority.

What Does Zero Waste Mean?

If you want your head to start spinning, plug this into your web browser and start reading. This term has been evolving and been redefined over and over as the years pass. The truth is it depends on who you ask. Here are some high-level, brief examples:

1. Responsible production, consumption, reuse and recovery of products, packaging, and materials
2. Encompasses the entire product lifecycle including design and disposal to minimize environmental impacts
3. Diverting waste stream from landfills
4. Waste minimization, avoiding landfills and incinerators
5. No discharges to land, air, or water that threaten the environment or human health
6. Producing no waste

7. Conservation of all resources and strive to minimize waste generation

It is easy to get confused by a bunch of well-meaning words here, so don't sweat it. We as average citizens can only control what we purchase and produce, what is brought into our homes, and how it is handled, so let's focus on that. My sustainability mantra is **Avoid, Reuse, Repurpose, Compost, Recycle, (Landfill).** With zero-waste entertaining, I stop at recycling and say no to landfill, and I work hard to avoid recycling as much as I can, as we discussed at length in chapter two.

It is much easier to accomplish zero waste when you have well trained troops. My immediate family and close friends have been through zero-waste bootcamp on many occasions and no longer look for the trash can they know is not there. They have each graduated from food waste management camp, being well schooled on the difference between greens and browns for the compost pile and what is recyclable.

The larger an event is, the more challenging this can be, but I will provide you with some tried and true methods that have worked for me over the years. In reducing waste while entertaining, you do have options. You can start small by reducing or eliminating plastics, or you can declare your event to be zero waste and ask your guests to embrace your mission. Do whatever works for you, knowing that it might take time before you get into a groove that is comfortable for you.

This is a journey that can only be taken one step at a time, and the reason this chapter is toward the end of the book is that it is a bigger step, requiring more effort and more investment than some of the topics earlier in the book. I didn't do this all at once, and you don't have to, either. Start with one or two things, then step back and evaluate the results. Sometimes you may need to adjust and try again. Now that you're in the right frame of mind, let's get this zero-waste party started!

Drinkware

Because I do not want to purchase beverages sold in bottles or cans as much as possible (beer seems to be the biggest exception at our parties, talk to my husband about that!) and we do not use single-use cups, we had to find an alternative. I attended a zero-waste event where the drinking cups were small jelly jars that were very cute and added to the atmosphere of the party. It was an aha moment for me, and my love of Mason jars was born! I prefer to use the larger 16-ounce jars and used them for a Fourth of July party. I bought canning labels so people can put their names on their cups, and I quickly learned that the canning labels work a little too well as they are a chore to remove. After trying a few other labeling methods, I've found that painter's tape works very well, and it comes right off when the party is over. Just throw them in the dishwasher, and store them in large, lidded containers to keep them clean between parties. There are some real advantages to using Mason jars for drinkware! First, they go with nearly everything— baby shower, Fourth of July, or Labor Day BBQ. Second, if you find that you need more, you don't have to worry about being able to find some in the same pattern or style. Finally, you can always use them for dry food storage or canning at any time. Mason jars are available in various sizes in most box stores, grocery stores, Amazon, almost anywhere you can buy food storage or cooking supplies.

To avoid plastic water bottles at parties, large attractive drink containers are readily available in acrylic or glass, and the Mason jars serve as the cups to be filled. These will last year after year, and you can get creative by adding lemon, mint, or oranges to provide a tasty and visually appealing drink for your guests.

Beginner: Buy compostable cups and compost them if that is available to you or buy recyclable cups and recycle them after the party. (This only counts as diverting waste if you make sure these get to the compost pile or the recycling bin; throwing them in the trash will only get them to the landfill!) If going the recycling route, avoid plastic and use an uncoated paper cup that will more readily break down when recycled. Make sure it is recyclable in your area.

Intermediate: Invest in reusable cups of your choice and reduce or skip canned and bottled beverages. Guests will consume what they are served, so you don't need to go crazy offering tons of options. Beer can be served in kegs, pony kegs, or from growlers. When having a party that others are contributing to, ask them to bring larger servings that can be shared.

Advanced: Invest in a few larger drink containers for water, lemonade, and any other items you regularly consume at parties.

Napkins

Zero waste means no paper napkins or composting the used paper napkins. Trying to get away from the cost and waste of paper, I was looking for a cute idea for a casual summer party, and an alternative to cloth napkins caught my eye, bandanas! They were perfectly festive, affordable, washable, reusable, and most of all, they don't create any waste. I placed a bulk order for a few dozen red and blue bandanas for the party, this was going to be great! At first, our guests were a bit confused, not quite sure what they were for, but they quickly adapted. What happened next left me confused. When it came time to pull them out for our next party, I noticed there were quite a few missing. That was weird, but I shrugged it off; then a pattern started to emerge. After every party, there were fewer and fewer bandanas, I couldn't figure out where they went. By the time we were planning one of my husband's big birthday parties, we were down to a handful. To this day, I don't know what happened to all those bandanas! Were my guests really taking them home? Maybe they thought they were gifts? Maybe it just reminded them of their high school days when the cool kids used to wear them on their heads or around the legs of their jeans? I was stymied.

It was time to do something different, so I invested in white cloth napkins, like the ones you get in nice restaurants. Funny, it has been years, and the white restaurant napkin population remains strong. Like Mason jars, they go with any occasion, theme, or décor. They were not particularly expensive and can be bleached if necessary. Because they are thick and sturdy, they hold up well over many washings. I may never need to buy them again!

Plates

Plates proved more challenging than napkins because of cost and storage considerations. I had a small set of nice dishes I bought for holiday sit-down dinners, but our holiday crowds were steadily growing to 20 or 30 people, and the summer and birthday parties were downright huge at 50 or 60 people. The holiday dishes were not suitable for our summer parties, so it was time to invest in more dishes. Both cost and storage being considerations, there was not much I could do about the size of a standard plate, but there was something I could do about the cost. Cue the local dollar store. I tend to forget how great dollar stores are. Over the years, I have found some incredible things for a very small price. On the downside, there is no guarantee what you will find on any given day, and I was looking for 60 matching plates. They had 60 plates, all suitable for a casual summer gathering, but some were blue, some were green, and some were yellow or orange. The assortment of colors and similar styles added to the fun of a summer gathering, so it worked out fine. What a deal, 60 plates for $60! Being sustainable doesn't have to cost a fortune. Just imagine how much money I've saved by using and reusing these plates over the years versus buying throw aways for every occasion.

I cleared some space in a high cabinet for storage of the excess plates when not in use; they could also be put in a lidded container and stored away in a garage or closet. For appetizer plates, I purchased sturdy plastic plates as we wash and reuse them party after party. I am yet to host a party where a large quantity of bowls has been called for, but if you come across that situation, I'm sure your local dollar store could be of assistance!

Beginner/ Intermediate: Start with reusing appetizer plates and gathering your plan for dinner plates.

Advanced: Add the number of plates you need to cover your next few gatherings.

Flatware

As our party crowds grew, we eventually got to the point of not having enough flatware to accommodate that many people. The flatware we had at the time was a horrid mishmash of different patterns, some of which I swear we never bought. Raising four kids, we had silverware disappear and reappear over the years—I'm pretty sure if I checked the drawers of their friends' homes, they would have some of ours and we have some of theirs. Maybe some of them ran off with the bandana napkins and the socks we never found in the dryer.

I took this opportunity to start anew and donated our odds and ends and bought a new matching double-sized set for our everyday flatware, then picked a different pattern for our party flatware that I store in the buffet with the holiday plates. The big summer gatherings usually only involve forks, so I went back to the dollar store and bought a huge supply of matching forks for the summer parties to fill out all the flatware needs. Unless the flatware starts conspiring with the napkins, we should be set for life!

Food Scraps

So far, we've been working on the **AVOID** and **REUSE** strategies, avoiding waste before it even happens in the planning process. Let's talk about **REPURPOSE** and **COMPOST** now that the party is happening.

Food waste of some kind is inevitable, whether it's from preparation or guest plates; little bits and scraps must go somewhere, and the trash or the garbage disposer are not our preferred options. Food scraps from big parties almost always include animal products like meat and dairy, so putting it straight into the compost pile is not an option. Instead, I use Bokashi. To be clear, *Bokashi is not composting,* but when done properly, you can put Bokashi food waste in your compost bin. If you put this term into your search engine, lots of people trying to sell you things will say, "Bokashi composting." Be careful here, you don't need most of what they are trying to sell you.

What is Bokashi?

There is some disagreement whether its origins can be traced to

Japan or Korea, but we all seem to agree that as with many cool things like herbal medicine and acupuncture, it originated in Asia. Bokashi is an anaerobic (without air) method that is used to neutralize food waste products so they can be composted or directly buried in the ground to nourish plants. Because the process is anaerobic, it can be used on meat and dairy products, as well as any other kind of food waste. A microbial inoculant is mixed with a bran product (can be various grain waste products, like spent grains from breweries, rice, or wheat), molasses and water, then fermented making Bokashi bran that is available for purchase, or you can make your own. The microorganisms colonize the bran that is then spread on the food waste. The bran then pickles the food waste, preventing rotting and making it unattractive for animals and pests.

Preparation

Materials needed:

- Airtight container sized right for waste you are planning
- Inoculated Bokashi bran

Since this method can mix vegetable matter with meat and dairy, it's my go-to choice for parties. I use a super sexy 5-gallon Home Depot bucket with a screw on lid for easy access ($12 setup from Home Depot—you must buy the screw-on lid separately), but any airtight container will work. I label the lid "Food Waste" and put it where people would expect to find a trashcan. Sprinkle some Bokashi bran on the bottom before the party starts, then periodically sprinkle a layer in as the food waste accumulates. When you are done adding, give it another generous sprinkle of bran and seal the lid tightly (remember, without air!) and leave it alone for at least 10 days. You can leave it alone for as long as you want, actually. I've left mine for months before doing anything with it and have not had problems if it was kept closed. If you want to see what is happening inside, use a clear container—it's fun to watch!

Bokashi Notes:
- This only works for fresh food waste. Do not add rotting waste to this process.
- I've had the best luck when I ensure that most, if not all, of the food has some bran on it.
- Draining is not necessary, though many retailers will sell the ability to drain a container as a feature. I have never done it, nor have I needed to. I don't add liquids to this process.
- It is normal for there to be white fluffy mold associated with this process.

Harvesting your finished Bokashi is simple. You can either add it as a green to your outdoor compost pile or dig a hole near a tree or bush you want to feed (preferably with 8-10" of dirt cover) and bury the Bokashi. Done!

Troubleshooting:
- There is black or slimy mold – something went wrong. I have had this happen a couple of times in my early tries. This can happen when you have a lot of food waste and do not include enough bran. Unfortunately, the only thing you can do is throw this in the trash. White fluffy mold good, black slimy mold bad.
- Smells – a good batch will have a faint fermented smell like a brewery. Foul smells mean something went wrong.

Beginner: Start with a small container and get the process down with some household meals.

Intermediate / Advanced: Go big and do it at your next party!

Recycling and Trash Containers

This is very important, so please pay attention – do yourself a favor and *remove all trash bins from the kitchen and food prep area before the party starts.* You will get some well-meaning helpers on party day, and if they don't know the system, food will end up in your trash can. If you leave trash cans out, you won't be able to keep up with monitoring them while entertaining your guests. I hide mine in a room where guests won't go and close the door.

If you serve any canned or bottled beverages, make sure you have well-labored recycle bins that are large enough for your crowd and you have several around in areas where they are most likely to be used. Most people are somewhat informed about recycling these days, and it makes things much simpler when there are only a couple of things that can be tossed into a recycle bin because you have created a zero-waste party!

Inform Your Guests and Recruit Some Help

It is an important step to inform your guests in advance that your party is a zero-waste event and explain what your expectations are in the invitation. For example, the invites for our Fourth of July potluck invitation might say something like:

"As always, all events at the Davis house are zero waste. Please do not bring any items that cannot be composted or recycled, and we ask that you take any leftovers home."

Asking people to take leftovers home ensures that they don't over contribute and bring something that they will enjoy eating later if there are leftovers. For an event where we are supplying everything to minimize waste:

"As always, all events at the Davis house are zero waste. We appreciate you being our guest and ask that you bring only your joy and friendship; we are happy to provide the rest."

Your frequent guests will catch on quickly, and your new guests will stop and think about what they intend to bring into your home. This is a bonus because you are now making someone else aware of everyday things they can do toward sustainability!

It is very helpful to recruit some well-trained help. I have a couple friends and family members that attend most of our parties and know the rules well, and they are always willing to pitch in on party day. They know the most important way they can help is where the most waste is generated, in the kitchen. They help with food prep and cleanup, making sure the food scraps from the guest plates end up in the right place.

A zero-waste party or event is achievable, we have proven this over and over. It does take some planning and tenacity and may call for an initial investment in reusable supplies, but in the end, I believe the benefits far outweigh the initial effort. Reusing is always less expensive than disposable items in the long run, and it is far friendlier to the planet.

Whether you do it alone, with some volunteer help, or you hire a crew to help you, zero-waste events are mostly about limiting choices. If you don't provide paper or plastic, people will use what you provide, and they'll be considerate of your efforts. If a recycling bin is available, they'll use it; and if a trash can is not present, they will ask what they should do. You will be a zero-waste party master in no time!

"Hey, Dee!"

Commonly-asked Questions

1. Hey, Dee: We don't do much entertaining, but we attend other people's events. What can we do?

   Being mindful of what you contribute to the party is a great start. If the host is providing everything, offer to take home the recyclables or compostables, or get ambitious and see if they are on board for you bringing a Bokashi set up for the party. Suggest a keg instead of cans and offer help planning and during the party.

2. Hey, Dee: I help out with some community events; how can I get them to make these events more sustainable?

   Tell the event planners and coordinators what you have learned about zero-waste entertainment. Call me or have them call me; I can help!

3. Hey, Dee: Doesn't washing all those reusable dishes use a lot of water? That makes disposables more sustainable, right?

   This is a common misperception. Earlier, we talked about all the water and energy used in creating single-use items, then more water and energy are spent transporting, recycling, or putting them in landfills. Composting uses 10x less water than recycling, and washing and reuse uses hundreds of times less water and energy over time. Reusable is more sustainable.

Avoid, Reuse, Repurpose, Compost, Recycle, Landfill

12 YOUR DOOMSDAY DASHBOARD

DRY GOODS * CANNING * DRYING * VACUUM SEALING * BULK BUYING * GROWING

Let me just get this out of the way—I'm into the doomsday prepper thing a little more than I would like to admit. I think I can blame my mom for this; she always had enough food in the house to feed our family for months, so I grew up thinking this was normal. I'm not quite sure why she did it, but I do know that we always bought in bulk to save time and money traveling back and forth to town. Living in the country, I know that my parents always wanted to be prepared in the event there was a power outage or weather-related incident. Maybe Mom just didn't like shopping, I don't really enjoy it either. I do know that Mom's tendency to buy in bulk and be prepared for a calamity rubbed off on me. If things go awry, I want to be sure that I won't run out of food after two or three days. I also don't want to find myself at the grocery store fighting with other customers over the last gallon of milk or loaf of bread. What is that about, anyway? We all know no matter where you live, if there is a threat of a power outage or storm of any kind, everyone rushes to the store for loaves of bread. People will clear out the shelves at the first mention of a storm, won't they? We can now add bottled water to that list.

This mentality also applies to warmer regions, believe it or not. When we lived in southern California, and there was a power outage that was expected to last more than a day, everyone freaked out and cleaned the store out of milk, water and bread. We won't even mention the great toilet paper hoarding of 2020 that struck the entire world. The compulsion to stock up in the face of a potential crisis is in all of us—perhaps it's a primordial instinct. Since that is my normal mode, I don't often find myself in panicked need of anything, except fresh food that can't be kept very long.

I don't like to shop, and I'm not one who drops everything to run to the store and snatch the last loaf of bread. I prefer to stay prepared— even when there are no predictions of storms, outages, or disasters. At all times of the year, I have a pantry / basement full of dried beans, rice, flour, sugar, pasta, and various other staples—enough to get us through Armageddon. I figure if things go south, I need to be able to feed my entire brethren (four kids and their spouses, and our grandchildren). Even if they're not prepared, I guess I feel it is my motherly duty to make sure we can all feed ourselves for a while.

My preparation also includes gathering heirloom seeds and starting to grow some of our own food. We will touch on growing food and preserving and storing large quantities of food. Being self-sustaining is a big part of reducing consumerism and living a sustainable life.

Dry Goods

Whether you obtain your food by growing, buying, or trading, once you have it, you need to figure out how to keep it fresh and on hand long term. Humans figured out the science of storing dry goods as soon as we started farming and staying in one place for long periods of time. Dry goods, or "staples" as they are often called, are an essential part of survival and self-sufficiency in lean times and when things come undone.

I have used many different methods for storing dry goods over the years, things as simple as an empty coffee can with a good lid to a Mason jar and everything in between that will provide a good seal for long-term storage. The key is to keep air and bugs out. If you have taken any composting classes from me, you know I love those big red Folgers coffee containers. Once they are done supplying coffee, they can easily be cleaned and used to store dry goods, like oats, rice, beans, pasta, sugar, and flour. Slap some labels on the top and sides of the cans (painters' tape and a Sharpie work just fine), and your staples are doomsday ready. Reuse is the name of the game! You can also purchase containers of various sizes that are specifically made for food storage at stores like Smart & Final, Target, and Amazon.com. If you take a quick glance into my pantry or basement, you'll see a mixture of all these containers.

PRO TIP – make sure your lid is snapped on tight. I failed to do this with a container of flour, and I have no idea where the bugs came from, but I had to throw out the whole container, consisting of probably two flour sacks. (Because flour + water = paste, this created quite an adventure in the compost bin until it decomposed.)

Canning

What nature-loving doomsday prepper would be caught dead without a pantry full of home-canned goods? At one point in my life,

I had never canned before, but I decided I wanted to give it a try. After talking with a few people who had experience, I decided to give it a whirl and see if I could make some jam. One year, we had a bumper crop of—you guessed it – fuzzy nectarines. Nectarines have natural pectin in them, so you don't need to add pectin to make jam. Just let them get to the peak of ripeness, chop, cook, and BOOM! You have jam. It's simply the easiest jam to make, especially for a beginner. Now to can it and preserve it for the future...

I was amazed at how easy canning is; I didn't have a single failed seal my first time doing it! I made about 16 jars, gave a few away, and greedily ate the rest. There is nothing like eating homemade canned jam. Unfortunately, the next year just as I was running out of jam, we lost all the blossoms to a windstorm, and I didn't get a single nectarine. This is what happens to any gardener: nature intervenes, and we are reminded that we are not the ones in control.

So, Dee, are you going to tell us how to do canning? Not really, but I will tell you a bit about what I do and provide some guidance. There are already many books and websites that deal with canning, and although it may seem daunting, it really is one of the easier things to do.

I will say that there are types of canning – water bath and pressure canning. Which you use is sometimes up to you, and sometimes up to whatever you are canning. Some things like fruit and some vegetables can be done in a water bath, no special equipment required, just a large pot, some water, and a burner. Depending on what you are canning, the time for the bath will vary. Other things like meat and certain vegetables need to be pressure canned and require a pressure canning device. It looks like a big pot with a lid and a steam rocker on top. Again, what you are canning will determine the pressure and time requirements, but this is also not difficult. A pressure canner will cost between $80 and $150.

Since getting my feet wet in canning, I have canned everything I can find. Jams, cooked beans, sliced fruit, hot peppers, cranberry sauce, tomatoes, vegetables, the list goes on. Anything goes, and with a hearty supply of preserved home-grown and home-cooked foods, I don't have to worry about having enough food to eat if the power goes out for a few days, weeks, or when the dreaded zombies take over. I really look at storing food as insurance against having to constantly go shopping or if there was a big life event and money become scarce at some point. The thought of not having food is not a comfortable one for me.

A note on canning classes, certifications, etc. I have never taken a canning class, nor do I have any certifications in canning. I can tell you that if you do take such a class, you will be told things that are ... somewhere between less than sustainable and simply not accurate in practice. I can only speak from my own personal experience and the experiences that others have shared with me.

1. Do I sterilize my jars? Yes, if I am using them for canning. For dry storage, I just make sure they are clean.

2. Do I sterilize my lids? Yes, if I am using them for canning. For dry storage, I just make sure they are clean.

3. Do I reuse lids once they have been used for canning? Yes, if they are not damaged and can still provide a good seal. The recommendation from the FDA is that the lids are used only once then thrown out. It is important to test the seal on each jar after cooling. If it does not seal properly, you can use the food immediately, or swap lids and try again.

4. How long do you keep your properly sealed canned goods? Years if the seal is intact. This is also not in accordance with FDA guidelines that recommend keeping sealed goods less than one year. I believe I have only lost the seal on one item in all the years I have been doing this. How did I know? I could see the mold growing from the air intrusion (ewww, right?). The contents went in my compost bin, I sterilized the glass and threw out the lid. How old is my oldest one right now? Maybe five years.

5. Do I sell my canned goods? Never. They are for consumption by friends and family only. I suspect that if I were to sell them, I would have to take the class, get the certification, and follow those rules.

6. Do I label it? YES … well, mostly. If you have ever looked in my freezer, you would know I am bad at labeling. I always think I will remember, but I don't! Do you know how many times we have had freezer surprise for dinner? Sometimes that is a hilarious adventure; one time, it was pie filling! As usual, my family is very patient with me. I have tried every method of labeling and what works the best and is the easiest is painter's tape and a Sharpie – no lie. The labels you buy at the store or online stick too well and won't come off, Sharpie on glass does not stay, and the next thing you use the container for might be totally different. Don't waste your energy or brainpower on this one, a roll of painter's tape and a Sharpie is all you need.

7. What should you do? As they say, "you do you, Boo". I am a firm believer in operating in your own comfort zone, especially when it comes to food. It will do no good to can a

basement full of food if you are not confident in your methods and are then anxious about consuming it. Your doomsday stash, your rules.

Don't forget to rotate your stash – use what you can and rotate the aging stuff out; nobody wants to crack open a jar from 20 years ago and hope it's still good. I try to put the newest ones in back and the older ones in the front, so we are using the older stuff throughout the year.

Drying Food

No doomsday prepper would be truly prepared without making sure they have plenty of dried (dehydrated) food on hand. I bought a food dryer for just this purpose. By the way, you don't have to buy a dehydrator – your oven and a cookie sheet will also work! My first experience using the fancy dehydrator was disappointing, mostly because I was so excited to see my results that I was too impatient to wait for the food to fully dry—it takes many hours in a dryer to dry food. You really can't be in a hurry when you are doing this. Depending on the food and its water content, it can take more than 12 hours to fully dry, and very juicy items like blueberries can take a couple of days. Once I learned to alter my expectations and select food for drying with this in mind, I loved it. And I realized just how easy and convenient it is—just put the food in the dryer and come back the next day to check on it.

I purchased a food dryer that is all stainless steel. I had to look far and wide to find one that was big enough and made entirely of stainless steel, and I had to pay a bit more for it. But considering how much I use it, it was worth it.

1. Size – when you put food into the dehydrator, it can take a lot of space, but once dried, it comes out very small. A lot of rack space is beneficial to hold the food, especially before it's dried. For example, my dryer has 10 trays, and I can fit about 8 or 10 big apples (sliced) in it. Once dried, though, the slices are much smaller, and in a couple days of snacking, my husband and I can wipe those out. Those same apples would sit whole on the counter for weeks and not get eaten! In our opinion, they taste even better dried. The drying process concentrates the sweetness and makes fruit irresistible!

2. Materials of construction – Plastics off gas when heated, depositing chemicals into food, so I don't like using the combination of heat and plastic with my food. There are silicon mats that come with the oven you could use, but I try and avoid that whenever possible.

3. What you plan on drying - Last year, I had so much extra squash from the garden that I started drying it. Now I have squash chips we can eat or add to soups, stews, or casseroles. That's right, once food is dehydrated, it can be rehydrated! That opens a whole new world of possibilities, while drastically reducing the size of containers and storage system you'll need.

4. Dry food storage – I mostly use my most favorite container – Mason jars! I can see what is in there, check to make sure it looks good, and I can fail to label it and will (probably) be able to tell what it is later.

Drying is great for herbs, as well. Each season, I pick fresh mint and basil and dry it for later use. The mint leaves can be used for tea or to add a little minty freshness to water or food. I crumble the basil straight into my soups, sauces, or meat. Dried basil can be used in the same way you'd use the dried basil found in jars in the store, but when it's homegrown and freshly dried, I assure you that it is exponentially better than anything you can buy in the store.

Vacuum Sealing

While we are on the topic of preserving food, let's talk about vacuum sealers—a perfect way to preserve food and space! There are two types of vacuum sealers: one seals food in bags, and the other seals jars. I know this might shock you, but I have both!

Vacuum sealing items that go into the freezer bags will prevent freezer burn by preventing ice from forming on the food, which frequently happens in the airspace that is left with standard storage. Vacuum sealing prolongs freezer storage, extending its "use by" time considerably, and it helps preserve natural juices and flavor, especially in meat.

Bag Sealer

I have used a couple of different kinds of bag sealers, but I have never used the most popular, which is Foodsaver vacuum film. The reason I have never used this kind is because it creates a lot of plastic waste. These sealers use a two-part plastic sheet that you cut, and the food is sealed between them. This single-use plastic is thrown away after just one use, and I just cannot support such waste. It is worth the effort for me to tell people that Foodsaver also has reusable zipper bags that can be sealed with a small handheld device that only costs about $50, which is cost effective, given that their large film unit costs about $200. In the beginning, they were not specifically marketing them as reusable (even though they were). As of this writing, they have improved the design and are marketing them as reusable. I strongly advise giving them a try, they work quite well, produce far less waste than the sheet style, and the sealing device is a fraction of the cost of the larger style. True, you will have to bear the cost of purchasing the bags, but they are very durable and can be cleaned and used many times.

Hey, Dee – do you reuse these bags even when you store raw meat?

Yes, I do! We have a stringent cleaning protocol at our house anytime raw meat is present. Utensils, cutting boards, knives, and yes plastic bags. Hot water and contact time with bleach followed by a rigorous cleaning with more hot water and soap has kept everything safe for many years. Please make sure you rinse everything very well whenever bleach is used on food contact surfaces.

Mason Jar Sealing

The goal of sealing food into Mason jars is to keep it fresh longer and prevent pantry bugs like ants, moths, beetles, and weevils that can infest flours, dried grains, pasta, rice, crackers, cereal, and other dried or powdered foods. Additionally, vacuum sealing extends the shelf life and freshness of food. Storing some items too long without vacuum sealing will affect the flavor of some nuts that are higher in oils, like walnuts or peanuts, if they are open and stay on the shelf for long. Walnuts that I have left too long become bitter to the point that they are unusable. I like storing these kinds of items in glass containers to eliminate micro plastic contamination, and the clear containers make it easy to see how much is inside. (I know what you are thinking – do you label it? Your guess is as good as mine!) With various jar sizes available, you can easily portion out what you are leaving open and in use, while leaving the rest securely sealed in the pantry or long-term storage area.

In the last few years, Mason jars have increased in popularity as self-sufficiency has gained in popularity. I have been a Mason jar freak for many years, using them for everything from drinking glasses to dry food storage and canning. For a couple of years, I have been seeing advertisements for automatic Mason jar sealers. Hmmm ... I admit I was intrigued, but I'm not typically an early adopter of technology – I like to let them work out the bugs and get some competition going to keep the price down before I dive in. The price point is $25 to 30, so it's not a large investment, but I wanted to make sure I chose a good quality item that was going to last and wouldn't add to the waste stream after a few uses. One feature that I was also set on was finding one that was either plugged or rechargeable, so I was not dependent on batteries that were going to become part of the waste stream.

I finally settled on one and purchased it (UNERVER corded with rechargeable battery from Amazon $28). Go to my YouTube channel and see how excited I was after the first day of using it! It worked GREAT, and I'm pleased to say that the seals have held flawlessly on both standard and wide mouth jars. So far, however, I have only used it for dried goods like spices, nuts, flour, rice, and the like. I have not used it for canning fresh foods, like jam or fruit. In addition, I cannot say whether these vacuum sealers are intended to be used instead of a water bath or pressure canner—it's still a little unclear to me. Until we have official guidelines, I would err on the side of caution and continue to water bath or pressure can fresh food. You can use the jar sealer to vacuum seal something fresh to prolong refrigerator storage. Heed this warning, though: the vacuum is rather strong and when you pop off the lid and the seal is broken, sometimes things slosh out or even pop across the room, so be careful if you store anything liquid. I've had the same thing happen when breaking the seal on a jar of rice—typically, a few grains do come flying out like Mexican jumping beans!

And the hidden bonus? When you know your shelves are stocked, you get to kick back and relax while everyone else is rushing to the store to participate in the bread, milk, and water melee.

Bulk Buying

Another strategy for money saving self-sufficiency is bulk buying. Many of the things we talk about in this chapter require space, and I realize that not everyone has an abundance of space, but you can get creative. A closet with some shelves in it, crates, or totes also work well. Sometimes, I split bulk buys with a friend or family member. This cuts down the cost obligation, as well as the storage space required. Growing up, we bought everything in bulk, from gallons of milk to sides of beef and whole hogs.

There are many places you can buy in bulk; the trick is finding what is available near you. If you have never been to a bulk store, I urge you to plug that into your search engine now! You can try things like "bulk buy, bulk store, bulk food, or refillery." Just because you are not aware of these stores does not mean they aren't near you – you may be surprised! If nothing is available near you, Nuts.com is a great resource and will deliver straight to your door. Nuts.com has become a local go-to source for me to buy bulk oats (I buy 25# bags at a time) and mixed nuts, which are awesome snacks and awesome chopped up in my homemade granola. They also sell dried fruit, flour, spices ... and the list goes on. They also have a good variety of gluten-free items!

One day, I was in the bulk foods section at my local Sprouts grocery store, and I asked if they would allow me to bring in my own containers. The manager said yes, bring them in and we will weigh them empty for you and take that weight off at the register. Jackpot! The next time I went there, I showed up with a cart full of empty containers. They did as they promised and weighed my empty containers for me. I attracted quite an audience in the bulk food aisle that day, filling containers with oats, ground flax, pumpkin seeds, and several types of beans. Other customers were very interested in what I was doing and stopped to ask me questions about how it worked and what kind of containers I like to use. I was giddy with excitement when I left that store! That was a fantastic day!

I have found many stores offer certain foods in bulk. Some of the ones I know of:

1. Sprouts Grocery Store
2. Natural Grocers
3. Smart & Final
4. My Patriot Supply (survival kit style food)
5. Nuts.com
6. Pleasant Hill Grain

Some refilleries also have bulk food options. Pleasant Hill Grain is a great resource for large quantity, long-term storage. Their five-gallon Super Pails have airtight lids and oxygen absorber packets, creating an oxygen and bug-free environment inside the pail until you are ready to open them. Now, if that's not a doomsday must have, I don't know what is! They also offer many self-sufficiency options for canning equipment and food preparation, like bread makers, presses, grinders, and slicers.

We can't leave the topic of water out of this chapter. Bulk water storage can be tricky, but we will be in big trouble with no clean water to drink far before we will be in trouble with food. The choice of most preppers is water purifiers. Each of my family members have been gifted Life Straws, and I have several backups for emergency use. These have a built-in filter made for hikers that allows you to drink directly from a water source like a stream, removing all water borne bacteria and micro plastics. They are very reasonably priced at around $25 or less each and claim to filter enough water for one person for up to 3 years, I have never tested this claim. Considering this could allow you to drink water you would die without, I think $25 is a pretty good deal. Another water strategy is to buy large containers of water and rotate them periodically. If they are in an airtight-sealed state, and remain unopened, they should be good for some period of time, but I am not sure if I would test that out in years. My water stock remains sealed, and I date each container (again with the Sharpie – I swear they are not paying me to say it). I have stored water containers for just over a year, and they have been fine. I use the dates to rotate the stock, drinking the older ones and replacing them with newer ones. Caution—in cold climates, stored water is subject to freezing, and what do liquids do when they freeze? Expand, so think carefully about where you are storing the water, and when possible, leave a bit of space for the liquid to expend if Jack Frost comes nipping.

Growing

There are shelves of books dedicated to gardening methods, and they are written for various regions, so I will provide some guidance but not a complete guide here. **I highly recommend that you don't wait until there is a crisis to start your food growing adventure.** This takes some work, dedication, and practice, so don't expect 100% success your first time out. Any gardener would agree that even with years of experience, not every garden does what you want it to every year. We like to think we are in control, but really nature has the reigns!

What works for you may be different than what works for someone else, so give yourself some time and some grace here. For example, I always seem to do well with hot peppers, but most of my neighbors don't. Establishing a bartering system in your area for trading food from your gardens is a great way to get rid of extra produce and get something you didn't grow or was not successful for you. I run a bartering page in my area for this very reason!

1. Get into the zone – Determining your planting zone is crucial as it will determine when you can first plant and what kinds of things you can grow. Type "planting zone by zip code" into your search engine bar and you will find numerous resources to answer that very question. The USDA planting zones break the US into 11 areas. The zone I currently live in is 5b, but I used to live in 9b, and gardening in those two places is very different. One note of caution: the zones are based on average temperature differences between your zone and the next, so they can change over time! If you are near the border of a given zone, in a few years, you may find that the zone boundaries have changed, so check back occasionally.

2. Location, location, location – When planting outside, finding a proper location to plant is essential. Many varieties of edible and fruiting plants require a lot of sunlight. If you are not able to plant outside, never fear, there are many options for you to grow inside!

    a. Full sun – you are best off in a full sun location. Many edible plants such as tomatoes, peppers, onions, peas, etc.

like warm soil and a lot of sunlight. Is there such a thing as too much? Yes, but that is what shade cloth is for.

b. Soil – If your soil is like mine, it's not suitable for planting. I have raised planter beds with good soil and compost for my garden. We built our own raised bed planters with UNTREATED wood (this is a very important note. Do NOT use treated wood for garden beds, or anywhere if you can help it. Treated wood will resist rot and bugs better, but it's injected with toxic chemicals that will seep into your soil and ultimately your food and water supply). I got a garden mix in bulk from a local soil supplier, as well as a very large load of compost and mixed those together. I also spread leftover compost all over the existing clay soil about 2-3" deep in areas where I was going to plant later. This helped break up the clay soil and ready it for planting next year. Made a HUGE difference!

c. Planter beds – We built our planter beds. (Okay, let's be honest here—even though I was a carpenter in a previous life and was fully capable of building my own planter beds, my sweet husband did it for me. So, when I say we, I really mean Mike.) I designed them to be 4' wide and 8' long, 12" deep. The lumber was 2"x6"x 8' stacked on edge to make the beds 12" deep. They don't need to be any deeper for root growth, and you want to limit the width so you can reach the middle from either side. Length can be anything you want; we chose 8' because that is the standard length for wood.

3. Indoor growing – If you don't have the outdoor space to grow, this does not mean you are left out of this conversation, it's just different. You can and I have grown year-round in my basement. I know people that do it on their countertops, in their living room, or in a spare bedroom. Actually, growing indoors makes a lot of things easier. You don't have to worry about bugs or critters getting to your plants. There are no grasshoppers, rabbits, or squirrels. There's no wind, hail, or freezing temperatures to damage your crops. What it does require is light, and lots of it.

   a. Lights – there are all types of lights available these days to grow indoors. My basement grow room has wire racks and grow lights rigged up on them, along with heating mats to help with sprouting and continued growth for warm soil plants. Typically, I do my starts in the basement, then move them outside except for lettuces / greens, which I keep in the basement year-round. (Let me tell you, homegrown greens are incredibly full of flavor compared to what you buy at the store!) A cool thing I learned AFTER I bought all my lights is that standard cheap shop lights like the ones you see in a garage work fine for growing lights. You can really save yourself quite a bit of money by not falling for those overly expensive fancy grow lights. I do have to admit my basement does look pretty cool glowing purple at night, though! Whatever kind of grow lights you are using, the plants need many hours of light per day (like 12-16), so energy efficiency is a key factor. If you are doing starts, adjustable height is needed as the light needs to be relatively close to the soil. I use a system of chains and S hooks to adjust the height of my lights on the rack.

b. Hydroponic growing – there are many kinds of grow towers and other hydroponic systems that can be used indoors to grow food. My sister had a little tabletop one where she grew greens in her little condo—worked great for her. These come in various sizes and levels of complexity based on your needs and desire for investment and volume of food. Some of the smaller versions come with lights, but many don't, and you will need to put them near a window or add light. Plants typically get their nutrients from the soil, which is why good soil is so important; however, no soil is used in hydroponic growing, only water and liquid fertilizer. Large scale hydroponics (aquaponics) use fish waste from fish actively living in the water to provide the plants nutrients in the absence of soil. Small scale hydroponics typically use liquid chemical fertilizers. I recommend a little caution here—these are chemicals that are feeding your food that you will eventually consume through eating the plant. I am not a hydroponic gardener, but a little research has revealed that not unlike gardening in soil, the nutrients that can be used in hydronics are similar – bone meal, fish meal, and animal fertilizers. The only fertilizer I use in my garden is fish emulsion – it's basically pureed fish and smells like it. I assume you could use some of this liquid in your hydroponic system, but I could not promise that your house will not smell like fish. I recommend some heavy research here, followed by some fun experiments!

With so many ways to preserve and store food, it's easier than ever to check off all the boxes on your doomsday dashboard. When you grow your own or preserve fresh food, you will be eating healthier, unprocessed food that you know is safe and good for you. When you buy bulk and store and grow your own food, you are greatly reducing your waste footprint on the planet. Think of all the ways you are reducing your impact:

1. Less trips to the store, less gas is spent going to the store saving time and money.
2. Less packaging required for the items you buy in bulk, no packaging for items you grow.
3. Less packaging and food waste entering the waste stream.
4. Less transportation cost hauling away the waste stream, less trash / recycling pickup.
5. Never have to worry about food security for your family.

Avoid, Reuse, Repurpose, Compost, Recycle, Landfill

CONCLUSION: YOUR JOURNEY, YOUR WAY

There you have it—your sustainability journey has begun! Whether you implement one thing or several of the sustainability measures in this book, I applaud you! Anything you do, no matter how small, will make a difference.

As you continue your journey, I encourage you to remember the story of the little girl on the beach, patiently tossing one starfish at a time back into the ocean. YOU are that child, choosing to make a difference one tiny step at a time, one better habit at a time, one little change at a time. There is no guilt or shame the Self-Paced Sustainability way!

It has taken me decades to integrate all the measures in this book, and I am still learning, growing, and adapting—from the products and packaging I choose, the habits I adopt, and the new methods I try. No matter what you choose, whether you're partying down zero-waste style, raising happy worms, or cooking delicious meals with the power of the sun, there will always be new things to learn.

Follow me as I continue to learn and grow on my journey. Please join the Self-Paced Sustainability communities listed below, and ask me your questions, share your practices, insights, ideas and implementations, and help our sustainable community grow and live in concert with the natural world.

Join the Self-Paced Sustainability movement for information, tips and tricks at:

Facebook Group: Self-Paced Sustainability
https://www.facebook.com/groups/1558400145090374

LinkedIn Group: Self-Paced Sustainability
https://www.linkedin.com/groups/14484969/

YouTube:
Yellowstoneprofessionaled https://www.youtube.com/@yellowstoneprofessionaled

LinkedIn:
Yellowstone Professional Education
https://www.linkedin.com/company/yellowstone-professional-education/

Instagram:
Yellowstoneprofessionaled https://www.instagram.com/yellowstoneprofessionaled/

Podcast: Management Under Construction
https://podcasts.apple.com/ca/podcast/management-under-construction/id1790081339

www.yspe.co

Sign up for our mailing list: https://bit.ly/4iHmjXL
Email: heydee@selfpacedsustainability.com

I look forward to connecting with you!

Dee M. Davis

SELF-PACED SUSTAINABILITY RESOURCE LIST

The following resource list is based on products that I have personally tried and can say have worked well for me, as well as a reminder of other types of places similar items may be found. The ZP / LP rating is based on the packaging that I have received when ordering. I provide links directly to the manufacturer where possible; many of these products are also available on Amazon or other online or local stores. I have received no compensation from any vendors on this resource list.

ZP = zero plastic, ZPO = Zero Plastic Option, LP= less plastic

Chapter 2: Recycling is NOT the Answer!
Reusable Flatware Set w/ Case – Arroyner reusable stainless steel – Amazon (ZP); local zero-waste store

Chapter 3: One Starfish at a Time, an Approach to Plastics

Soap Bars/ Shampoo Bars: Ladybug lather https://www.etsy.com/shop/ArtisanHandmadeSoaps (ZP/LP); local artisan, zero-waste store or refillery.

Tooth Cleaning: www.simplysooney.com tooth powder (ZP); Huppy toothpaste tablets www.behuppy.com (ZP), local zero-waste store or refillery.

Toothbrush: Virgin Forest Bamboo Toothbrush – Amazon (ZP), local zero-waste store.

Deodorant: www.littleseedfarm.com (ZP), local refillery or zero-waste store.

Laundry soap: Tru Earth laundry strips https://tru.earth/ (ZP), local refillery or zero-waste store.

Cleaning Supplies: Branch Basics www.branchbasics.com (ZPO) they offer glass or plastic bottles. (This is one of the few truly effective nontoxic cleaners available.)

Food Storage Containers: Pyrex https://pyrexcontainer.com/ (LP)

Toilet Paper – Scott Professional 80 rolls – Amazon (ZP), Amazon Aware 24 roll – Amazon (ZP)

Chapter 6: Start Bugging Your Bugs

Fish Emulsion: https://indian-river-organics.myshopify.com/

30% Vinegar: Harris 30% vinegar - Amazon

Chapter 8: Now You are Cooking!

Solar Ovens: All Season Solar Cooker by Sol cook https://www.solcook.com/ (ZP), MrMapMax 4.5L portable – Amazon (LP – some packaging)

Chapter 9: The Lazy Composter

Totes: https://www.rubbermaid.com/containers-totes.html

Compost Crank: https://www.lotechproducts.com/products/compost-crank-compost-aerator (LP)

Compost Bin: https://algreenproducts.com/collections/composters/products/soilsaver-composter (Recycled plastic)

Chapter 10: Happy Worms

Worm Condo: https://eartheasy.com/worm-factory-360-composter

Red Wiggler Worms: https://unclejimswormfarm.com/ (ZP/LP)

Chapter 11: Let's Get this Zero-Waste Party Started!

Cloth Napkins – Utopia Home 24 pack – Amazon (LP – may have some packaging)

Bokashi Bran: Formerly Bokashi Brothers, now Dr. Jim Z https://drjimz.com/products/bokashi-fermented

Chapter 12: Your Doomsday Dashboard

Canning: Pressure Canner www.gopresto.com (ZP)

Drying: www.Magicmillusa.com (LP)

Vacuum Sealing: UNERVER M11 vacuum sealer – Amazon, www.foodsaver.com (bags and handheld sealer)

Bulk Buying: www.nuts.com, www.sprouts.com, www.costco.com, www.smartandfinal.com, www.naturalgrocers.com, www.mypatriotsupply.com www.pleasanthillgrain.com

ABOUT THE AUTHOR, DEE M. DAVIS

Author, Consultant, Subject Matter Expert, and Educator are but a few of the arenas in which Dee brings her sustainability knowledge and expertise. Sustainability has been at the forefront of Dee's life since the beginning and has blossomed throughout her life in unexpected ways over the years. She is passionate about reducing waste, and conserving resources, and living in concert with the natural world. Dee has earned numerous certifications as a leader in energy management, environmental design and construction, sustainable behavior, composting, and conservation. She shares her knowledge as an instructor, coach, author, and consultant with people across the US and around the world, specializing in making even the most complicated topics simple.

Dee is also the author of the children's book series, Mara Meets, releasing the first book in the series, Mara Meets Sandra's Sweet Rolls, in 2024 with several more in the works. She is the owner of Davis Consulting Management Group and Yellowstone Professional Education. Dee has lived in various states across the US and currently resides in Colorado.

Where you can find Dee:

Self-Paced Sustainability (Facebook and LinkedIn groups)

Instagram: @yellowstoneprofessionaled

LinkedIn: https://www.linkedin.com/in/dee-davis1/

YouTube: @yellowstoneprofessionaled

Podcast: Management Under Construction, co-hosted with Bradford Wyant

Visit her website www.yspe.co to learn more.

www.ingramcontent.com/pod-product-compliance
Lightning Source LLC
Chambersburg PA
CBHW070628030426
42337CB00020B/3950